the Red Magus

Other projects by Natasha Joy Price:

———————————————

Freedom of the Soul
Balm to the Soul

The Red Magus

NATASHA JOY PRICE

Copyright © 2024 by Natasha Joy Price

All rights reserved. No part of this publication may be reproduced, distributed or transmitted in any form or by any means without permission of the publisher, except in the case of brief quotations referencing the body of work and in accordance with copyright law.

ISBN 978-1-916529-27-4 (paperback)
ISBN 978-1-916529-28-1 (ebook)

The Unbound Press
www.theunboundpress.com

Hey unbound one!

Welcome to this magical book brought to you by The Unbound Press.

At The Unbound Press we believe that when women write freely from the fullest expression of who they are, it can't help but activate a feeling of deep connection and transformation in others. When we come together, we become more and we're changing the world, one book at a time!

This book has been carefully crafted by both the contributors and publisher with the intention of inspiring you to move ever more deeply into who you truly are.

We hope that this book helps you to connect with your Unbound Self and that you feel called to pass it on to others who want to live a more fully expressed life.

With much love,
Nicola Humber

Founder of The Unbound Press
www.theunboundpress.com

For Olivia, Alice, and Thomas.
I hope you clearly hear your Soul's wisdom.

Foreword

Natasha and I first met nearly 20 years ago when we were both attending a local development circle. Here our joint interest in all things esoteric saw us forming a friendship which endures to the present day. A thirst for knowledge in both of us, to understand not only the world around us but also the unseen world, that which could be felt and experienced on some levels but not fully understood, led us to past life regression. We undertook our training together to become Regression Therapists with the Past Life Regression Academy with great excitement (and probably a little naivety) about how life-changing the course and our adventures in past lives would be. Together we have explored many of our own past lives, understanding their relevance in our lives today, uncovering unexpected connections and witnessing firsthand the impact the understanding and healing of these memories our souls hold has had on our lives, ready for us to move forward with a deeper awareness of ourselves and those around us.

The Red Magus is a skilfully written adventure realistically showing the depths of understanding that our past lives hold for us, those links reaching through time and space which can trigger us to confront problems in our current life and also heal those to gain understanding of our purpose and lessons, as those from past lives may still be relevant in our current life. Throughout lifetimes we can incarnate with the same souls, often in different relationships, seeking to gain completion and forgiveness. This book is a shining example of the power of revisiting these lives along our soul continuum, in understanding all of our soul's experiences and how we can utilise the skills and knowledge that we acquired before we came into our current human existence.

Alongside past life regression, Natasha has skilfully woven into the story her experience and knowledge of many healing modalities, including Reiki and the use of crystals and oils. Although this story is fictional, it has drawn on many years' experience of other people's and her own past life journeys, showing the healing journey that can benefit us all if we are open to it. Past life regression reaches deep into our soul, taking us back to the source of an issue and usually to a place that we would not have chosen were we writing the story. By tapping into the plethora of memories our soul holds within our subconscious, we can gain an understanding of the lessons from those times and their relevance to our current life today, letting go of repeated patterns that can be holding us back. By reaching backwards we can gain the understanding and the healing that we need so we can move forward in a positive way, just as Cassie does in this story.

I was honoured to be asked to write this foreword for Natasha's first fictional book and I hope through reading this that it ignites within you a desire to explore your own past lives: all of the wonderful stories of the lifetimes you've led, the people you've met and the adventures you've had; the learnings gained and skills that you can bring forward, so that you can evolve into the most perfect version of yourself by utilising everything that is part of you.

I can honestly say that once you start your own exploration and adventure into your past lives it will open up a whole new meaning to your life today. I hope it's an adventure you undertake with a kind and wise guide, who can help you heal where needed, to understand and move forward as Cassie does in this beautifully written novel. So thank you, Natasha, for bringing Cassie's story to life and presenting it to the world, opening the eyes of all who read it to perhaps go on their own journey into past lives – they won't be disappointed!

Tracey Harley
Regression Therapist
Past Life Regression Academy
Trainer & Director of Supervision

Introduction

My spiritual path started almost twenty years ago with a Reiki session. I had just given birth to my third child, and the weather was extremely hot, a combination which gave rise to very swollen ankles. My mother suggested that I go and have a Reiki treatment with a friend of hers called Rosie. I had no idea what to expect but went along needing some relief from the swelling, with my newborn son in tow. I don't think I relaxed at all throughout the time I spent with Rosie, being nervous as to what was going to happen and always conscious of where she was in the room, but I did feel the energy, and see coloured lights throughout the healing. During that session, I also had a strange experience, which could have frightened me but, in fact, absolutely fascinated me and made me want to find out more about this Reiki energy. I immediately wanted to know where this energy came from, what it was made of, and how I could use it for my own health and wellbeing. The questions whirled around my head and started my journey of discovery – which has now been going for almost twenty years.

To learn more about energy work, I studied Reiki with Rosie and eventually went on to become a Master and a teacher. I also studied a variety of healing modalities such as Karuna and

Introduction

Lightarian Reiki, Theta Healing, Crystal Healing, and I gained a Masters in Parapsychology and eventually a diploma in Past Life Regression Therapy. I read and studied as much as I could, soaking up the information and understandings that came my way. My discovery of the ability for us to travel to past lives and clear old patterns, thoughts, energy blocks and ancestral beliefs was mind-blowing to me. I even discovered that you could change past lives and rewrite them, resulting in energy and emotions being released, and a shift occurring in your current life. This shook my beliefs, thinking and understanding to that point. I felt that as I took on board all the new concepts and ideas, the walls of the paradigm of my life at that point fell. My understanding of who I was in the Universe changed. I loved every moment of it.

I then discovered Future Life Progression and realised that you can travel forward in time, both in this lifetime and to view future lives. I also discovered the concept that time is not linear, but that all our lives are playing out at one time, which explained why things were not static in past lives but could be shifted. Eventually, I came to understand that we can move around the path our Soul has taken, or our Soul Continuum, in any direction, collecting information and knowledge, and experiencing deep healing. It was life-changing to be able to explore my energy in this way, and the beginnings of *The Red Magus* began to form in my head. I wanted to include as many spiritual themes, concepts, and ideas as I could to not only add depth to the story but to introduce readers to the things I love and have found incredibly helpful over the years.

Throughout this time, I continued to work as a solicitor in the

Introduction

corporate world, which was stressful and hard work, but very rewarding and enabled me to fund my children and lifestyle. The two areas did not always seem to flow well together, but by using my energy therapies and techniques, I have found a way to stay in a very centred and balanced state and for the pressures of the corporate world to not overwhelm me. I have also found my journey fascinating and entertaining, and wanted to share with others what is possible with energy therapies and how working with your own energy field, or Soul Continuum, can provide much-needed wisdom and information. *The Red Magus* was born. It has taken time but been great fun in the process, and I continue to enjoy all aspects of energy work. I hope this story will entertain you, introduce you to ideas and concepts, and allow your imagination to let loose as to what is possible when working with energy.

Acknowledgments

To my past teachers, and my past students, who have taught, nurtured, and tested me, but without whom I would not be the therapist, author, and podcaster that I am.

To my children, family and friends who have loved and supported me whilst I travel my spiritual path.

To my wonderful parents, Raymond and Georgina Price, whose love and support I have known throughout my life.

To Susie Smith, my teacher, friend, and energy peer.

Cassie

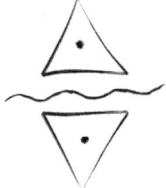

Cassandra Brooker-Jones stopped to look up at the tall white Georgian townhouse and tried to locate the bird that she could hear. It was a harsh repetitive call and, almost immediately, she saw it perched on the branch of a tree, at the side of the building. The bird was large with shiny black plumage and seemed agitated, flapping its wings as he hopped from one foot to the other. She wasn't sure whether he was a crow or a raven but as she listened to his shrill call, both of her hands went to her upturned coat collar, which she pulled up further around her neck, protecting it from the cutting wind. A doubtful quizzical expression played on her face as she pushed the black iron gate open and made her way up the paved path to the front door. The front garden was beautifully tended to with some purple shale in a central square and exotic-looking plants staged around the edges, also wrapped up tightly in sheets of plastic at this time of year, as protection from the cold. It was a very smart house,

Cassie thought. The furrows in her forehead deepened slightly as she reached the dark blue door, and she placed a hand on her stomach to stop the fluttering sensation. She noted the knocker was the head of a bird, like the one announcing her arrival, as she pressed the doorbell. As the resulting chime echoed around the hall, she stepped back slightly, seemingly anxious as to who was to present themselves to her, which made no sense as she knew Sara quite well now. When Sara answered the door, she had a broad smile on her face and Cassie immediately relaxed, smiling in response to the warm welcome she was receiving.

As Cassie stepped into the hall, Sara gave her a big hug and then ushered her down a flight of steps into the large kitchen which ran through the basement, the full length of the property from front to back. Sara busied herself making a warming cup of tea for them both, whilst Cassie perched on one of the tall chairs running along the large central island and breakfast bar. The kitchen was predominantly white, making the most of the light that was able to penetrate the basement, and Cassie took it all in with an admiring glance. Whilst Sara emptied some biscuits onto a plate and arranged cups and saucers on a tray, they chatted about husbands, their children and life in general. Once the tea was brewing, Sara, carefully carrying the tray, led the way upstairs into her treatment room at the back of the house.

It was also a large open room, but this time it had a full wall of glass overlooking the garden. There had obviously been an extension at some point, with the original rear wall of the house being extended out, and floor-to-ceiling windows being put in place. The blinds were half down creating a room of light and shade even in the dull winter weather. A small table light in one corner of the room cast a warming circle of yellow light across the navy-painted wall to the side, on which was a ladder of wooden wall shelves extending up almost to the ceiling. The rest of the room was painted in various shades of cream, and this made the darker wall stand out even more dramatically. On the shelves were an array of crystals of all sizes. Some were the size of a football, whilst others were just small tumbles, but all seemed to glint slightly in the glow of the lamp. They were a mixture of colours which Sara had arranged in order from dark to light, creating the effect of a wave of ombre colour sweeping across the wall.

'Wow!' said Cassie as she stood mesmerised by the effect.

'They're beautiful aren't they,' Sara agreed, 'and all natural colours which just fascinates me.' She came to stand next to Cassie and they stood looking at the crystal wall for a few seconds together in silence, admiring the beauty of it.

The bottom shelf – positioned at waist height – was different as it contained a vast array of little brown bottles together with a round white plastic container. 'What are these?' Cassie asked Sara, picking up one of the bottles and scanning the label.

'They're my essential oils, and this is the diffuser that I use,' Sara advised her, pointing to the white container. Sara opened the lid of the diffuser, revealing that it was already filled with water, selected two of the little bottles and let a couple of drops of each fall into the container, then replaced the lid and pressed a button. 'These oils are frankincense and neroli, and both are particularly good for deep meditation so it will help you as we relax and go into trance,' Sara stated.

A plume of what looked like steam tumbled out of a slit in

the side of the lid, as the beautiful aroma filled the room. 'Ooh that's lovely,' Cassie said, sniffing the air.

'Come and sit down and have your tea,' Sara finally prompted as she sat on the large navy sofa set at a right angle to the navy wall and patted the seat beside her. Cassie took a seat as she was told sinking slightly into the comfy cushions, whilst balancing her cup of tea carefully in one hand.

'Thank you,' she said, smiling at Sara. 'I'm a bit nervous, to be honest.'

'Oh, don't be,' Sara reassured her. 'There is nothing to be nervous about. We will just see what comes up for you. And you trust me, don't you?' She smiled leaning forward as she did so, and Cassie realised that she did indeed trust Sara and the process that she was so obviously passionate about.

She smiled back and nodded, 'Of course.'

About an hour later, having finished their tea, as well as a full explanation from Sara as to what to expect from a Past Life Regression session, and Cassie having completed the client questionnaire provided to her, Cassie found herself lying on large navy and cream toning floor cushions covered with a predominantly navy tartan blanket. As Cassie waited for the session to begin, she looked up at the ceiling. *What am I doing?* she thought to herself.

As Cassie drifted down into relaxation, Sara carefully led her through an induction and into a past life.

'He's going to stab me; he's going to stab me! Someone please help me!' Cassie's body began to shake uncontrollably with the well of emotion suddenly flooding and overwhelming her senses. The tears began to flow unchecked down her reddened cheeks and she was unable to hold back the deep sobs as they spluttered in rapid succession from her cocooned body.

She could hear Sara's soft slowed voice as though from a distance. 'It's okay, just allow the tears to flow. The emotion you are feeling is only energy being released. It's all normal and okay, you're very safe. Nothing can happen to you now, it's just a memory.'

Sara's attempts to soothe Cassie's rising angst did not seem to make a difference as the furrows in Cassie's forehead contorted and deepened, and her hands – gripping tightly over the edge of the blanket – remained in place.

'Just allow the emotion to be released, allow all that energy to flow out of your body.' As the sobs continued with no sign of abating, Sara came to sit on the floor at Cassie's side and took her hand, encouraging her to open her eyes and to come back into her treatment room, back into the here and now.

As Cassie opened her eyes and focused on the kind smiling face of her therapist and friend, the sobs began to quieten slightly and she visibly relaxed. After a generous pause, Sara spoke. 'So, tell me what was happening for you?'

Cassie took a few deep breaths, trying to gather all her wits about her so she could try and explain what she had been seeing in her mind's eye and the intense feelings of fear that had overcome her.

'I was running away from a man. I think he was my brother, well that was what came into my head anyway. I'm not sure how I know that, but I just do.' Cassie looked up into the face of her friend for reassurance and Sara nodded at her in an understanding way.

'He was looking for me in this building full of pillars, but I felt as if he was hunting me.' A sob caught in her throat as she seemed to be searching for and picking her words carefully. 'I'm confused though. If he was my brother, why was he trying to hurt me?'

Sara gently ignored the question and encouraged Cassie to tell her more about her experience. 'Just explain to me what you could see and what was happening.'

Cassie, still lying on the floor cushions covered by a blanket, allowed her free hand to finally relax and come to rest by her side, whilst still holding Sara's with the other. She breathed deeply. 'I was running through what seemed to be an open-air courtyard, with open corridors down either side. The sun was bright and causing all sorts of shadows to bounce around. It was difficult to see because of the contrasts, but I could feel this menacing presence behind me, like someone was chasing me. The whole experience felt unnerving.' Cassie paused as she selected the right words. 'I felt like… no, I know that he wanted to hurt me.' Cassie paused again, wide-eyed, and gazed into space as she recounted the story. 'Yet, I could feel this confusion in him. I don't know how I know this or how I could feel his emotions, but I feel as if he was torn. Although he was trying to hurt me, he also didn't want to. He didn't really want to do whatever he was doing, but he was going ahead with it anyway. I don't really understand that but that's how I feel.' She turned to look at her friend. 'I think there was also a conflicting part of him that wanted to protect me.'

Sara gently smiled at Cassie. 'That's okay, don't try to force the information to come to you, just relax and we'll see what else comes up. When you are ready and if you are happy to do so, I want you to go back there.'

Cassie nodded, took a deep breath, and closed her eyes.

'I want you to breathe gently in through your nose and out of your mouth. That's it, just focus on your breathing and let your body relax again, back to that scene that we've just left.'

After a few minutes, and once Cassie's breath seemed to slow slightly, Sara asked, 'What's happening for you now?'

Cassie's closed eyes flickered slightly as she drifted back down into trance. Back to that beautiful sun-washed courtyard that felt so light and so in contrast to the emotions that coursed through her. She could feel herself ducking and diving behind the stone pillars which ran along each side of the square. She could hear her quickened breath and felt tendrils of fear beginning to creep through her. The building was like a Grecian-style villa with pale rough sandy walls and a terracotta tiled floor. The open-air corridor around the edge was formed by a red brick wall, with open window-shaped spaces above overlooking a central square. Cassie could see that a few of the bricks were crumbling in places and looked as if they were made of mud rather than modern bricks. She could also see that a few of the floor tiles had a motif or pattern on them in dark blue and she made a mental note of the design so she could recall it later. There were pots of flowers in the courtyard and placed along the half wall of the corridor so that you had to peep through the foliage to see beyond in places, and Cassie could hear the relaxing gurgling water sounds of a fountain playing somewhere. On Sara's instruction, Cassie looked down at her feet and slowly became aware that she was wearing natural leather sandals with ties crisscrossing up her legs, almost to her knees. It was a strange mix of senses that slowly brought the scene from the depth of her subconscious into her current conscious mind, a mix of seeing, hearing and just knowing. A delicate weave of energetic threads that slowly and gradually created a scene in front of her mind's eye. Following further gentle prods from Sara, she could also 'see' that she was dressed in a long soft yellow dress, tied at the waist with a belt that resembled rope. Her long wavy dark brown hair was loose down her back, but she could feel that it was clear of her face at the sides of her head and assumed that it was held up in some way with clips. There was a row of gold bangles up each of her arms and she could feel a necklace secured with a thick piece of leather which kept catching against her neck as she moved, but she couldn't quite make out the shape of it.

As she darted along the inside edge of one of the corridors, shafts of sunlight kept hitting the scene like searchlights from above, causing everything to flicker and strange shapes to morph on the walls behind her. The play of light confused her senses and made it even more difficult to 'see'. The whole scene was flickering in and out of her awareness as she struggled to grip it more firmly and the contrast of light and dark made it very uncomfortable.

'What emotions are coming up for you?' she heard Sara ask in the background. Her voice still sounded muffled as if she was far away and not sitting by her side in the same room.

'Fear, real intense fear. I know he's after me and that he wants to hurt me. I'm trying to hide but I know he's getting close and that he's going to catch me.' The gentle sobs started to bubble back up louder and louder until eventually they exploded out. 'He has a knife; he's going to stab me!'

'It's okay, it's okay,' Sara's voice rose to meet that of her client's. 'Just breathe deeply. You are safe and okay,' she reassured Cassie. 'If it's too difficult for you, you can float above it and view it like an observer, or open your eyes.' Sara allowed a couple of minutes to pass to see whether Cassie needed to open her eyes, but when she didn't she said, 'Tell me what's happening now.'

Cassie could not go on. She felt so confused as to what she was seeing, believing that it probably wasn't even real, yet the emotions were strong and washing over her in rapid waves. She could not remember when she had felt this level of fear before or when she had last let herself cry. The inconsistency of the light and the fact that the scene itself was uncomfortable and mixed with the immense emotion was becoming almost unbearable. 'I can't do any more,' she sobbed.

'It's okay,' Sara's voice soothed. 'Open your eyes now and come back into the room for me. Just breathe deeply and relax. Hold my hand, you're perfectly safe. It's okay, you are okay.'

As Cassie wandered the aisles of her local supermarket a short time later, having picked Xander up from the babysitter, the imagery of the session kept coming back into her mind's eye. Her head had started to ache slightly now from the tension and all the flickering light, but parts of the session remained clear in her memory and the fear that she had felt still lingered menacingly in the background. She felt as if it was hiding from her but allowing her to sense its presence, and that it could step forward at any time, wrapping her in its tendrils again. She shivered slightly feeling unsettled and in unfamiliar territory.

Cassie had known Sara for several years now and although she was aware that Sara was incredibly spiritual and had trained as a Past Life Regression Therapist, she had not really understood what that entailed. Sara had always been friendly, but the two had not really developed a closer bond over the last couple of years. Sara had just been one of the gang, the group of friends who occasionally met for drinks with snatched evenings of chatter and relaxation between work, family and children.

The group which Cassie regularly met was a mixed bag and included Alice, who was a university friend, Megan, a relatively new acquaintance who Cassie had met through aqua natal classes, Sara, who was Megan's school friend and the reason why their connection had not been particularly strong until now, and Emma, who had been a work colleague of Cassie's before going on maternity leave and eventually leaving her job. Cassie and Emma were both lawyers, although in different disciplines, and Cassie could not cope with the stress of the job once Xander had arrived and she'd realised the effect that being a mother had on her life. When she listened to Emma telling her the latest gossip and office upsets, as well as the stress of the job, she knew that she had made the right decision to leave. She certainly didn't miss the office and the thought of trying to juggle a stressful job and a baby was almost too much to bear.

After a few drinks one evening, Sara had explained to the group about her spiritual beliefs and how a session of Past Life Regression Therapy could play out. Cassie had felt incredibly drawn to her and to experiencing what she was describing.

Cassie could feel Sara's passion for her work and trusted her abilities. She realised that Sara always appeared very calm and at ease with her life, often holding space for the others as they went through a crisis or trauma in their lives. Why she suddenly now felt such a pull towards her, she didn't know, but that feeling of connection and that need to go further with it nagged at the back of her mind until an appointment had been made for her first Past Life Regression therapy session.

As Cassie pushed her trolley through the supermarket aisles with Xander secure in the built-in baby seat, she realised how shocked she felt by what she had seen and heard in the session. Shocked that she had been able to see a past life so clearly and at the strong emotions that had arisen making her cry for the first time in months. She wrestled with the idea that it was not a past life at all but something she had seen in a film or read in a book. Her conscious mind stepped firmly into her thoughts questioning her experience and making her feel a little silly. Yet a part of her argued back. The emotions had felt so real. That intense feeling of fear and trepidation made her think it was indeed a long-lost memory, deeply locked away in her subconscious. That fear had been powerful, the sense of foreboding incredibly strong, and the mere thought of it made her shudder again.

Cassie caught a glimpse of her reflection as she passed the free-standing fridges holding milk and juices, and her shoulders physically dropped. She felt deflated as she stared into her own eyes and felt the tears start to well up again. She did not like what she saw at all. She felt so fat and unhealthy. To anyone viewing Cassie from the outside, she was tall and slender and even though she had gained quite a lot of weight since pregnancy, she was still a good shape. Her tall stature allowed her to carry off the extra weight with no real effort. Her dark brown hair was straight and today held up in a pink cloth scrunchy, so her heart-shaped face was clearly visible. She wore no make-up, her skin clear and pale, but her hazel eyes were hooded and tired. She had always liked the fact that she and Joel had the same-coloured eyes, matching irises as well as the amber flecks within them. This similarity had been a source of teasing among their friends, although this was really the only thing that visually connected them.

Since the birth of Xander she had struggled to get back to her normal weight and the constant cycle of dieting and failure had begun to really deplete her store of motivation and confidence. She had never been fully confident even before Xander came along, being happy to allow her husband, Joel, to take the lead in most things, but now she felt almost incapable of tackling any task. She worried incessantly about everything and anything, and now of course the worrying about Xander and being a good mother just amplified her insecurities.

Cassie's thoughts naturally moved to Joel and his reaction to Xander's birth. He had been ecstatic about his new son. She remembered the room being full of his excited, happy presence. His energy was bubbly and upbeat, filling the space and infecting everyone who entered. It had felt amazing, but now he never seemed to be home and that just added to her list of worries.

'Oh, excuse me! I am sorry,' Cassie apologised to the fellow shopper as she swerved around her, narrowly missing her feet with the trolley. 'Miles away,' she explained and smiled faintly, lowering her eyes with embarrassment as she swiftly moved her trolley down the aisle to the checkouts.

She wished she could borrow some of that bubbly energy from Joel. Her energy levels were low these days. She wondered whether he still loved her.

Cassie finished the shopping without further incident, although deciding what to buy was becoming incredibly difficult for her. It just seemed so much effort week after week, trying to find something different to cook. The process would trigger a chain of insecure thoughts like a spiral of negativity and hopelessness about whether Joel liked her cooking, whether she was a good wife, whether she was a good mother, and all the time she would find herself wanting. The process was always the same, mentally beating herself up with taunts of what an awful person she was until she would be physically shaking with the crescendo of worry, stress, and anxiety as she walked to the car.

As she drove the short distance home, her thoughts were never very far from Joel. He had felt different lately whenever he was at home, and the thought that he may be drifting away from her seemed to mockingly laugh in her mind. Her stomach flickered slightly, and her heart beat a little faster with the mere acknowledgement of it. She loved him dearly and she knew she would not cope without his presence in her life. She also knew it was all her fault. He was her structure and support and had been for so long.

Cassie took a deep breath to stop the tears and resolved to make more of an effort, to lose the weight, to dress nicely and to generally be more upbeat. He could not possibly leave if she was smiley and happy, she thought. She practised smiling at herself in the car mirror, a lacklustre attempt and felt her eyes stinging slightly again. She knew she was not happy, but she just didn't know what to do about it or how to resolve her situation for the better.

Once Cassie was home and had put away the shopping, she fed and changed Xander and laid him down for a nap. He quickly fell asleep, his dark loose curls spread across the cot mattress. She smiled lovingly at him as she wound one of his curls gently around her finger. He will need his first haircut soon she thought. The tears came again as her love for him almost overwhelmed her. She had to bite her lip from sobbing out loud and waking him up. Xander stirred slightly and Cassie backed away from him, tiptoeing around the toys to the bedroom door so as not to wake him. She slipped out of the door and pushed it gently closed. Leaning against the hall wall she sobbed quietly. She had no idea what the matter was. She cried when she felt unhappy, when she felt happy, and then again for no reason at all that she could determine. It felt as if all her emotions were becoming blended together to form one soggy helpless mass.

Eventually, Cassie was able to pull herself together and headed quietly to the kitchen. Whilst she waited for the water in the kettle to boil, she rummaged through a pile of papers in one of the kitchen drawers before pulling out a pale blue notebook with a large unicorn motif taking up the whole of the front cover. The unicorn's horn was embellished with multicoloured sequins which always made her smile. Cassie smiled again now as she looked at this mythical character, remembering how one of her friends had given it to her one day to cheer her up. It had been shoved in this drawer for weeks, but Cassie now knew what she could use it for. She turned to the first clear page, wrote the date at the top, and then recorded her experience from the session.

She wrote down everything she could remember, including what she had seen, and then added every emotion that she had felt. Underneath she wrote out everything that she had just known even though there was no reason for it and added a question mark. Had she made these parts up just to fill in the gaps and make a good story? She nibbled at the end of her pencil as she mused over this thought. Cassie wrote 'BROTHER' at the bottom of the list and underlined it heavily. Why would a brother be trying to hurt his sister? As she leant on the kitchen worktop, she started to make a separate list of all the reasons she could think of:

Jealousy.

Rivalry.

Greed.

Protection.

As she looked at the list of words she had written, she drifted off into a daydream, still standing in her kitchen but reliving the scenes that she had seen before, running through the whole experience step by step. Suddenly, something jumped out at her, and she started, standing upright with a jolt.

The motif on the floor tile. She could see it clearly in her mind's eye again and immediately bent over her notebook to draw it while she could remember it so clearly. She could recall two triangles, one upright and one pointed down. Between the base of each of them was a gap and through that was a wavy line. In the space of each of the triangles was a circle with a dot in it. As Cassie recalled the image, it seemed to fade from her awareness almost instantly, and she found herself questioning whether it was correct. She no longer seemed to have any reference to compare it with, as she struggled to recall the motif again. The act of drawing it had made it simply fade to nothing in her mind. It was a strange image and Cassie did not know whether it meant something, or whether it was just intended to be a pretty geometric pattern. She stared at it for a few minutes before shutting the notepad with a thud.

Joel

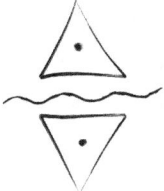

Joel Brooker-Jones wandered slowly back to the office, winding his way through the throngs of people enjoying the cool but sunny weather. He was a tall slender man with large hazel eyes and a mop of dark curls inherited from his Portuguese mother. The hair at the back of his neck and around his ears was cut short to balance out the additional weight on the top of his head, creating a modern well-groomed impression. He had turned the sleeves of his smart white shirt up in a casual fashion, revealing a long purple birthmark which ran along his left forearm from elbow to wrist. It had been an embarrassment to him when he was much younger, but now he thought nothing of it.

Joel was a confident and handsome man, with an engaging lopsided grin which was usually displayed easily and readily. However, today was different. He had enjoyed his lunchtime walk but his thoughts were brooding and difficult. He felt confused and torn and did not know what to do with the situation which presented itself. He loved his wife and child very much and was very aware of the importance of a loving family around him, but he felt an incredible physical attraction and emotional pull towards Ava. She was so pretty and friendly. It was easy to talk and laugh with her and being in her presence made him feel free again, as if there were no longer any responsibilities weighing him down. He had noticed how his energy seemed to change when she was around. Joel was aware, but completely unable to control the fact, that the way he moved and spoke changed slightly in her presence as if a light was being switched on within him. So much so that he always worried that the shift in him would be felt by others and give his true feelings away. The first time he had seen her he had the strongest feeling that he already knew her, although he was sure he would remember if they had met before, and when he was finally able to chat to her it was so easy and comfortable. It was like they already had history together, an understanding of each other and how they ticked, and he could see that she felt the same. He wanted Ava to be in his life in a romantic way, but the consequences of that action were massive and frightened him if he allowed himself to think about them too long.

Joel was not a heartless man. In fact, he was quite the opposite, with a massive respect and love for his family bred into him by his loving parents and very stable childhood. But Cassie seemed such a different woman now to the one he had married. She had always been quiet and shy, never wanting to be centre stage and he had liked that at first. So many of his previous girlfriends had been loud and opinionated, and Cassie was such an antidote when he first met her. He had always felt protective towards her somehow, wanting to soften the hard childhood that she had experienced and show her what a loving family could really be like.

They had known each other for years and that familiarity felt comfortable and easy. Joel had brought Cassie home from university one end of term to stay for a few days, and she and his parents had bonded instantly. It was as if she was a long-lost relative and there had been no awkwardness or uncomfortable silences. In fact, it was already like she was one of the family even back then, and Cassie and his mother, in particular, had formed a quick and easy bond. However, since Xander's birth, it was almost as if Cassie was reverting to childhood herself in some ways. She did not like to go anywhere on her own and using the telephone had become such an issue for her. He had once witnessed her visibly shake when he had pushed her to make a telephone call, believing it was just a case of getting her back out there and doing things. However, he quickly realised that her reaction was not normal. She appeared consumed with anxiety and did not like speaking to anyone.

Over those initial months of having a newborn baby, Cassie was incapable of sorting out any task, no matter how small, other than looking after her son. Her focus was, of course, on the baby, and although she appeared to be doing a good job, nothing else was possible and he would often return home to exhaustion and chaos. Joel could feel the irritation rising in him as he thought about how her behaviour had changed since Xander's birth. He had often tried to help and to raise her spirits, bringing flowers home and taking the baby from her so that she could get some rest, but nothing seemed to have worked. He felt so inadequate that his presence and actions did not make her feel safe and secure, but also, paradoxically, resentful that she was leaning on him so heavily. He felt such a failure as a husband and father. Admitting that thought to himself hurt and he had to shake his head to avoid the tears that were close to flowing.

By the time he was back at his desk, Joel's frustration and irritation had turned to anger towards his wife. He knew logically that it was not her fault, but the anger rose in him like a billowing grey cloud. It spread upwards from his feet, darkening his whole energy body, causing a heaviness to envelop his demeanour. If Cassie was not prepared to make any effort in return for his attempts at making her life easier, then why should he try so hard to help her?

Joel was incapable at that moment in time to realise how flawed his thinking was. He continued to struggle with anger issues and when in a clear-headed state of mind, he was calmly able to explain how the billowing grey mist just seemed to clog his logic and thoughts. However, Joel found it increasingly hard to experience and control this sensation.

It did not happen all the time by any means and his childhood had been in the main happy and loved. He had been a normal playful youngster, working his way through primary and secondary school with plenty of friends and success. Joel always showed a flair for sports, playing football in a succession of school teams, and had done well for himself academically. He particularly loved history and had avidly paid attention to those lessons, eventually going on to study Ancient History at university. Joel always loved playing with soldiers and war memorabilia, building up a collection of random war items as his wage allowed, an activity fuelled by his father, Patrick. It was a joint passion and Joel felt fascinated by the stories and accounts of battles and bravery, no matter which era or age they were referring to. He sometimes wondered whether the anger was somehow connected to his love of fighting and battles. There seemed to be an obvious link between the emotions he felt and how he imagined he would feel in such a battle, but he could not fully grasp how that connection existed. His father was also fascinated with the history of battles and yet was the most laid-back person that he knew, so there could be no real connection, he reasoned. Patrick had also emphasised the strategy of battles when he was young, teaching Joel how to think ahead, and to try and get into the mind of your opponent to win a fight. An aspect that Joel found fascinating and which he often used to his advantage in his subsequent career. However, the flashes of anger frightened him when they came. They were like lightning streaks flashing across his body, illuminating everything for a split second and then vanishing as quickly as they had appeared. It was in that split second of light that Joel lost all control. He had no resistance or willpower as that sensation overtook him. It was literally a flash point which occurred and which he could not recall once it had dissipated. However, the minute that he was on the other side he was able to see the results of his action: a broken car window; his roommate's guitar smashed to pieces; a colleague's broken nose. Luckily, he had been able to talk his way out of the predicaments he had found himself in, and no charges or further legal issues had arisen. However, he had lost friends and his family were more than aware of this angry trait. Joel knew he had been lucky so far as to how things had played out after these events and felt genuine shame at his actions. He had always believed that he could manage these emotions, that there really wasn't a problem, and when the thought arose that they were slowly increasing in number and severity, he would quickly talk himself out of asking for any help. His family had offered to get him some assistance after every episode, encouraging him to talk to someone and hesitantly suggesting counselling or alternative therapies. The resulting angry rebuttal from Joel always caused trepidation and they were afraid to push him too much in case a further episode would arise. Joel could see the concern and fear in their eyes and played on this somewhat in order that they would drop the subject and leave him alone. The shame he felt never subsided though and he strongly resisted delving more deeply into that pit of emotions and the root of his anger.

Cassie had witnessed Joel's angry streak several times but the first was the most shocking. It had been a couple of years into their relationship, whilst the two were still at university, and they had gone with three other couples to a local pub which held monthly live band evenings. The band playing, a local group consisting of three long-haired lanky teenagers, was awful but the banter and laughter had been genuine. The group had been made up of university friends and their partners, and they had spent a lot of time together over those academic years. Joel had been on particularly good form that night, the life and soul of the party, chatting and laughing with everyone at some point. Cassie had been enthralled with him and kept catching herself just watching him. She loved this man dearly and she couldn't believe how lucky she was that he was interested in her.

The argument started over nothing, just the different recollections of two friends and another argument which had happened in their first year of university. The details were not important but somehow, they gradually became the most important element, both men were unable to let go of being right and the relaxed atmosphere began to tighten and become brittle. A sideways smirk and a throwaway comment resulted in a broken cheekbone and bruised ego as Joel's friend found himself flat on his back, as the force of the punch knocked him and his chair backwards. It happened so quickly that a few of them did not even see it. Cassie was one of those. She had been laughing and chatting to Anna who was sitting to her left and saw only the resulting commotion as Rich lay sprawled on the floor his face red and already beginning to swell. They had all gasped and moved quickly to his aide but even at that point Cassie had not realised the real reason for the rapidly swelling face. It was only as the others started pointing fingers and looking at Joel with bewilderment on their faces, that Cassie cottoned on. She was horrified and confused. She had never seen Joel act this way and was truly baffled.

Cassie put it down to stress and reconciled herself with the fact that Joel was incredibly busy with essay deadlines coming up. She played the facts repeatedly in her mind, and always came out giving Joel the benefit of the doubt. Of course, Joel had apologised profusely, begging Rich for his forgiveness which was readily given. But over the following months, Cassie and Joel saw less and less of Rich and his girlfriend, and eventually, they were out of their lives for good. For Cassie, it was merely a one-off regrettable incident. However, if anyone had sat both Cassie and Joel down at that point and produced a graph showing the angry incidents in Joel's life, from birth until the present day, they would have seen a menacing incline. The incidents were slowly and surely getting more frequent. A black billowing gigantic cloud was rolling in, enveloping Joel and those around him. It was only a matter of time until it completely blocked them from view.

As Joel allowed the angry thoughts about his wife to reverberate around his head, he absently twirled a pencil around his fingers and swivelled back and forth on his office chair. As he did so, his gaze landed on Ava. Joel had a prime position to view the entire open-plan office from his desk and he often took a sneaky glance in her direction. He watched as nonchalantly as he could as she wafted across the floor from the other side of the building. He guessed that she was heading to the neat little kitchen tucked away in the left-hand corner of the office, and he got up to follow her. 'Waft' was a perfect description for the way that she moved, he thought as he casually followed her progress. She was so petite and light on her feet that she did appear to glide across the floor as she meandered through the desks, smiling, and saying a few upbeat greetings to her colleagues as she passed.

Joel joined her in the little kitchenette, making himself look busy as he asked, 'How are you today?'

'Good, thanks,' she replied softly.

'Usual time and place?' he asked as he let his hand brush hers without even turning to look at her.

'Cool,' was the reply, and he knew from her voice that she was smiling.

As Joel made his way back to his desk, trying not to spill his coffee, his thoughts drifted back to the first time he had seen Ava at a work seminar which the office had organised the year before.

Joel seemed to remember that it was about time management, but to be truthful he had not taken in anything that was said as he was too busy letting his imagination run wild with thoughts of the stunning redhead across the room. He had fallen for Ava almost on sight, her copper-coloured tresses causing most men in the room to take a second glance. He had been so taken aback that he hadn't had the courage to approach her, but a couple of days later an opportunity arose for drinks after work and he couldn't believe his luck when Ava turned up with a couple of her workmates. She was even more attractive up close and to his delight, Joel discovered that she was easy to talk to as well. They chatted for a couple of hours and by the time Joel had walked with her to the taxi rank, there was real chemistry between them and a knowing that something more was going to happen. And it had.

Over the next few months their secret meetings had intensified in number and life had settled into an exciting series of furtive glances and clandestine meetings. On several occasions, Joel needed to travel to see clients which required staying overnight and, of course, Ava would meet him there. It was easier that she came to him as she had no partner to deceive, and she would regularly travel to Joel's location for dinner, or to spend the night with him. Nobody would need to check her whereabouts, but if they did the similarities with Joel's would have been very apparent.

Joel had loved those evenings, returning to his hotel after a hard day's work, to find Ava waiting for him. Ava who was able to help him fully relax and yet feel energised all at the same time. Ava who often made him laugh out loud with her silly remarks and jokes, making him feel genuinely happy, and Ava who made him feel sexy and exciting.

It had been easy for him to gradually imagine being with her on a permanent basis and that thought had crossed his mind often, although he had not had the courage to voice it. On one occasion, although Ava had booked into the same hotel as Joel under her own name and in a separate room, the receptionist had called her Mrs Brooker-Jones by mistake. An electric pulse had coursed through Joel as she said it, making his stomach leap a little and they had both dissolved into a fit of giggles like silly school children, trying very hard to behave but feeling giddy with pleasure. Of course, on his arrival home to Cassie and Xander, the dark cloud that followed him would descend again but this time it would be tinged with red ribbons coursing through it, which Joel began to associate with guilt and a crippling shame for his behaviour. Sometimes he couldn't quite understand the magnitude of the dark emotions that enveloped him, to a point that he would need to gasp for breath and could hardly function. The effect that the emotions had on him seemed completely out of proportion to what he was doing. Although his affair was not honest or moral, it was not so momentous that he was almost paralysed to carry on his life when these emotions coursed through him, and tears often flowed.

It appeared to be getting gradually worse over time and Joel felt panicked by what he was feeling on more than one occasion. He had sought help with what he described as 'severe anxiety' and had been given several tricks to help him control it, and although they did seem to help, he was scared at the gradual escalation. He was also worried as to where it would lead and what it meant for him and his family.

Sometimes as a boy, Joel would have dreams of fighting. He was in a battle of sorts, fighting on foot in strange uniforms, and he could see and hear the actions of both sides surrounding him. It was during these dreams that a sword or knife would always cut him, exactly where his birthmark ran, from elbow to wrist. In his dreams, there would be blood and pain, and he could cry out, often waking himself in the process. He would wake back in his childhood bed, drenched in sweat, and clearly upset. His parents would comfort him and tell him it was just a dream and had no importance in his life. His mother would scold his father for the battles they had played out in the garden shed; she blamed him for scaring their son. His father would just retort that Joel had a vivid imagination and it wasn't hurting the boy. However, Joel remembered for a while that the time spent with his father talking about all things military and practising battle manoeuvres together had stopped.

Then as a teenager, when he was more able to express his fascination and wishes to spend time with his father, they started playing and strategizing with their soldiers again, and his mother was powerless to stop them. They would just laugh at her concerns and vanish to the garden shed for a couple of hours, much to Sophia's annoyance. However, she was also acutely aware and pleased that they were spending valuable time together as father and son, so didn't pursue the issue very hard. It did bother her though, and over the years she had begun to think that there must be a link somehow. Anger and fighting clearly were connected but she had no idea how to pursue that possibility, and she knew that neither Joel nor Patrick would cooperate with her in resolving it, so it had been left.

Now the dreams were back, stronger, and more vivid than before. Joel would see vivid images of war in his mind's eye, as if he had been there, as if they were memories stored in his subconscious rather than a dream. He would often hear the noises, feel the dust in his throat and nose and the men shouting and screaming. He would wake confused and frightened at what he was seeing. At times, what he saw made him angry at the injustice of it. At other times, he felt shameful as to what he was made to do to his fellow man. Whenever one of these dreams arrived, Joel would feel out of sorts for a couple of days afterwards, as if old wounds and emotions had been stirred up. His arm would also ache somehow, although he put that down purely to his imagination. Gradually, after a while, the feelings and emotions would fade away and he would go back to normality.

Joel realised that the intensity of the dreams was increasing, and often coincided with the grey cloud descending, making it very clear that there was a connection. He knew that both were trying to tell him something, but he just didn't know how to start unravelling that, or who to turn to for help. His mother had nagged him over the years to attend Anger Management courses, which he had done on several occasions, but nothing had seemed to stop the flow of the dreams and emotions increasing.

He decided to look a little closer at what these images were telling him and decided to keep a dream diary. He internally scoffed at the idea, and certainly didn't tell anyone, but it was something proactive which had been suggested to him and he knew that some action, any action, had to be taken. Joel had found a notepad at work and had brought it home, tucking it down his side of the bed together with a pen, so that as soon as he woke, he could record the information before it faded. And so, slowly, the details of those images began to become clearer. Joel found it strange that as he set his mind to see more details, that was exactly what happened over time. Gradually, he could see more and more of the uniforms, the weapons being used, and the faces of the men around him. He particularly became focused on the dress of the soldiers and that they had their arms and legs exposed which confused him. He had always imagined soldiers as being well-protected and having heavy hard-wearing boots, but these soldiers weren't wearing leather boots at all. It became apparent that they had what looked like sandals on, and that a lot of them had foot injuries because of it. Joel also became aware that the sun was glaring throughout the battle causing the blades of the handheld swords to glint, momentarily blinding him at times. Those glinting swords stirred up strong emotions within him and often triggered him to wake, gasping for breath. At other times the battle continued until he looked down to see blood dripping down his arm onto the yellow dust below.

Eventually, he had enough detail to Google the uniforms and to try and see whether what he was seeing was factual or whether it was just a figment of his imagination. After some research, he began to believe that they were Greek soldiers but then his logical mind took over and he dismissed everything, tucking his pad on a shelf in his wardrobe and choosing to ignore it all for the time being. However, the imagery of the flashing light and blood-stained ground stayed with him, almost taunting him with their vividness.

Joel and Cassie were sitting on the sofa one evening – Xander was fast asleep on the seat between them, providing a perfect excuse to stay slightly apart. They were watching a crime documentary when Cassie said, 'What have you done to your arm?' Her eyes settled on his birthmark. Joel was surprised initially, he had not noticed anything visually different, but when he looked down the purple irregular shape which he had carried all his life, did appear slightly darker and raised. 'It looks angry,' Cassie remarked settling her gaze back to the TV screen.

That word startled Joel and he looked again at the raised purple skin. 'I don't know,' he said as calmly as he could, 'I don't think it looks any different,' and he turned back to the TV as if to dismiss her observation. However, he knew that she was right, and he knew there was a connection between his dreams and his birthmark. He had avoided seeing it before or even thinking that it was possible, but he knew at that point, without any doubt, that his injury in his dream was the same as his birthmark. Don't be so stupid, he shouted silently at himself in his head. How can that be?

From that evening and that realisation, Joel noticed that his birthmark often looked angry and ached, causing him to rub his arm without thinking at times. It was as if his arm was also trying to get his attention in this whole mixed-up scenario, but Joel – for the life of him –couldn't work out what any of it meant and just felt lost and confused. The only antidote to these feelings was his time with Ava. As the dreams increased, so did their meetings.

One Friday evening Ava had driven after work to meet Joel. He had intended to drive home but had instead informed Cassie that he couldn't possibly get home that night as he was just too tired to drive, and it would be dangerous for him to try. Cassie was, of course, understanding and advised him to stay in a hotel somewhere and to get home safely the following morning when he was refreshed. She had suggested that he text her as he left, and she would have brunch waiting for him. Joel had felt so guilty at that point that he could hardly speak but assured Cassie that he would let her know when he left. He sent his love to her and Xander before slowly disconnecting. With a heavy heart, he had made his way to the local pub to meet Ava, but as soon as he saw her beautiful copper hair and wide smile, Cassie and Xander were pushed firmly to the back of his mind.

'Hi,' he smiled at her, 'was the journey okay?' Ava was already sitting at a quiet table, tucked away behind a wide oak beam. As he spoke, Joel pulled out the spare chair and sat down opposite her.

'Yes, all good. It was easy, to be honest. How was your day?' she smiled up at him, tilting her head to one side in a way that Joel found so attractive. Ava was wearing tight blue jeans and a vivid emerald blouse, with loose open sleeves, the colour of which clashed with but also highlighted her beautiful red curls.

'Oh, you know, the usual,' he said, trying not to stare at this striking woman in front of him. 'The deal with Murrayman is going well, we should have that in the bag soon which won't be bad for our figures this quarter.'

'Clever you,' Ava complimented him.

At that moment the waitress arrived, taking their orders, and replacing a couple of pieces of cutlery for them. A different waitress brought their wine, allowing Joel to taste it, before pouring them each a glass and leaving the bottle on the table between them.

'Cheers to Murrayman!' Ava raised her glass, and Joel responded in an exact reflection of her action, smiling broadly. He was doing well at work at the moment which was a satisfying feeling.

'Maybe I could work with you?' Ava ventured. She had never suggested working together before, but they had been getting on so well lately that she felt it might be her opening to plant that initial seed. 'What do you think Mr Brooker-Jones, would you be able to keep your hands off me!' and she laughed, leaning forward slightly, and smiling broadly.

Joel just smiled, tilting his head to one side this time, and raising his eyebrows at her. 'Maybe,' he said without offering anything else. Ava left it. That was enough she thought. A seed that hopefully would grow and help her with her plans.

Joel and Ava enjoyed their meal, chatting late into the evening before diving into bed for an equally hearty love-making session. Afterwards, they had cuddled and talked again, before drifting into a contented sleep. However, his vivid dream that night had woken Joel with a start, causing him to sit bolt upright, gasping for breath. For a few seconds, he struggled to fully shake off the imagery and emotions that coursed through him, shaking his head in a strange physical effort to do so. Ava had been instantly awake. She had never seen Joel like that and was concerned for him. He had called out in his sleep, and he was visibly shaking. She noticed the mark on his arm seemed to pulse slightly and she had to take a closer look in the gloom to be sure that what she was seeing wasn't just her imagination. The purple birthmark looked black in the gloom and Ava was slightly repulsed by the whole scene. Eventually, Joel was able to fall back onto the bedsheet muttering that it was just a bad dream before almost instantly falling back to sleep. Ava took longer to settle. The episode had unnerved her. She hated weakness in any form and something about his arm had made her feel very anxious.

It had taken her a while to drift off to sleep again, the events playing over in her mind, making her question their relationship and her motives. The next morning, they dressed and packed quickly with little conversation, before making their separate ways home. The mood was strained and uncomfortable and both welcomed the silent journey home with their own thoughts. A small crack had appeared.

The Magus

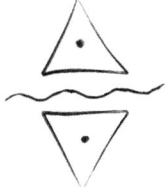

Cassie settled down on the large navy and cream floor cushions in Sara's treatment room, ready for her next session. She felt both anxious and excited about what was to happen and what she was going to see. The imagery of the first session had stuck very firmly in her mind's eye and she had been unable to shake off the feeling that her subconscious had led her to Sara, and that what had happened in that past existence was important and relevant to her now. In fact, the need to see and know more about what had happened seemed to have intensified since their last meeting. Cassie had a distinct knowing that she must unravel this information in her soul's path and fully understand it in order to help her in this lifetime. How, why, and in what way she had no idea, but she was unfaltering in the knowledge that she was going to follow this path that had been laid down in front of her and trust that what she would discover was beneficial. She snuggled down into the cushions, making herself as comfortable as possible, and wrapped Sara's lovely soft blanket around her as Sara's gentle voice began to lead her back down into the depths of her subconscious.

It was just darkness at first, but slowly parts of a picture began to appear, very faintly and briefly at first, like quick little snapshots being illuminated in front of her. If she didn't try too hard to hold onto them, they eventually became stronger and more complete, and Cassie was better able to accept the imagery that was being shown to her. Cassie marvelled at the way that she just knew some background details of what she was seeing with no need for explanation. The information just seemed to be there in her mind like a long-lost memory, which she could recall once triggered by the images she saw. As Sara took her deeper into trance, and Cassie relaxed even more into the experience, she could eventually make out the dim outline of a woman sitting cross-legged on the floor. The woman had a patterned shawl over her head which fell gently over her shoulders in relaxed undulating folds, and as she rocked gently backwards and forwards, the edge of the shawl kept obscuring the view of the woman's seated position. It was as if a light kept being switched on and off, creating an old crackling film effect, so that Cassie was only able to glimpse bits of the scene. 'What is it with flickering light?' the conscious part of her mind thought. Cassie could not quite make out any colours, the light was too dim, but she could clearly see the folds of the cloth and almost a rough handmade finish to the material. Cassie began to focus on the pattern, which was only visible in parts, as it was obscured by the folds, but she could see what appeared to be symbols running in parallel rows.

As Cassie took several deep breaths – on Sara's instruction – and continued to relax into the image, it intensified and came into focus. Cassie realised that the woman was doing something in her lap, focusing intently on the task in hand, with her head dropped forward. As Cassie continued to breathe deeply and tried to resist straining too hard to see, the scene in front of her suddenly rotated slightly and she could see that the woman was holding something, moulding it with her fingers as if shaping a piece of clay. She watched mesmerised as the woman continued her work, caressing the object as her body swayed gently back and forth in the gloom. Eventually, the woman straightened and placed the object on the ground in front of her. Cassie felt as if she was physically squinting as she tried to make out the details of what the woman was doing, but it simply was not clear enough for her to see. On Sara's instruction again, she relaxed and moved her focus to the room instead.

She was not sure whether the scene was set in dusky light or if the image of it in her mind's eye was not clear. It was difficult to see much detail at first but, eventually, she began to make out the uneven surface of the floor, with a rug covering the area on which the woman sat, and a rough finish to the walls as if mud had been thrown at them and then smoothed by hand. To one side, there were some rickety-looking shelves on the wall made from odd pieces of wood, and they were stacked high with rough, uneven food bowls, bits of candles, stones, and bunches of dried herbs. There were also little clay figurines and Cassie was sure that this was what the woman was making, but still, she could not quite make them out. Cassie focused on her breathing and tried to relax before concentrating on the clay items on the shelves. Suddenly one of them seemed to come into sharp focus. The image startled Cassie slightly, making her feel uneasy. It was the figure of a naked woman kneeling with her hands behind her back, clasped around her ankles and seemingly with her wrists and ankles bound together. It was not a comfortable image, but one which would appear to suggest restraint, even violence. Cassie turned her attention back to the figure the woman had placed in front of her on the ground and this time she could see that it was the same. The uneasiness began to spread across Cassie's stomach, making her feel quite nauseous.

As she continued to watch, losing track of time completely, the woman got up and fetched a small earthen pot from the other side of the room. It was rotund with a clay lid and the image seemed to focus in on the woman's hands as she handled the pot and reached in to bring out its contents. As she did so, Cassie noticed how young the woman's hands seemed to be. They were smooth, tanned, and dirty but had no wrinkles or age spots. Cassie could not tell whether this was the way that it was being shown to her, or whether the woman was in fact quite young. However, for whatever reason, Cassie concluded that this woman was not as old as she had initially thought. Cassie tried to focus in on the woman's face to confirm her impressions, but the shawl hung low over her head, and she was unable to make out any further details. As she concentrated on the edge of the shawl, however, long tresses of wavy copper-red hair slowly came into view. It was as if this was the only colour in a black-and-white scene, and the sight of the coloured hair caused a memory to flash across Cassie's mind. She acknowledged it but could not quite get the connection. She was sure it would come to her at the end of the session. She put it to one side as she focused back on the woman in the scene.

The woman drew out several needles from the pot – the needles also appeared to be of a copper hue. Cassie was again not sure whether this was her mind colouring the scene or whether the needles had really been copper or brass coloured. She didn't know much about these ancient times, but the colour appeared to be highlighted and significant to her subconscious. The woman carefully lined up ten of the needles in front of the little clay figure. She then placed several little glittery stones around the objects forming a circle and shaped a dent in the earth with her finger. She then reached into another misshaped earth pot and pulled out a half-burnt beeswax candle which she stood in the handmade dent. Cassie watched in fascination as she lit the candle by sparking two stones together, the light immediately forming a halo around the little scene. The woman began to rock again, which appeared to turn into a rhythmic flowing movement, leaning forward in the darkness and then arching her back before repeating the process. It was mesmerising and as she appeared to flow suspended in time and space, her hands moved in unison over the top of the figure in a rhythmic circular motion. Cassie had a sense she was chanting or reciting some words, but she couldn't hear anything or even see the woman's mouth. It was just an impression as if this woman was performing an ancient ritual, a ceremony of sorts.

Suddenly and without warning, the woman threw her head back holding her hands up to the heavens. Cassie started, physically jumping slightly with the surprise of the movement. She could clearly see the woman's face as the shawl slipped away.

The woman was indeed chanting or reciting something with her eyes tightly shut, and although they were screwed up causing her skin to appear crinkled, she was indeed young and very striking with her long red hair falling over her shoulders. Across her cheeks were symbols which looked black in the dim light, making her appear not only beautiful but menacing as well. As she finished the ritual her eyes snapped open and Cassie gasped, jumping for a second time. One of her hands flew to her heart which was now racing with the shock. The surprise and the physical movement caused Cassie to suddenly come back to the present day and the imagery disappeared.

Cassie lay for several minutes, allowing her breathing to gradually subside, and her heart to resume its natural rhythm. As Sara invited Cassie to open her eyes and come back into the room, Cassie noticed with surprise how calm and relaxed she felt. She should have been feeling anxious and unnerved with what she had seen, and had felt that way during the session, but in fact, now she felt clear and brighter somehow. She noticed that the vision of the wide, staring eyes of the woman was easily recalled as she discussed the session further with Sara, but instead of unnerving her or making her feel anxious again, it initiated a wave of warm relaxation. It was as if her subconscious was relaxed and at ease with what it had revealed to her. This reaction puzzled her.

Cassie and Sara discussed the session thoroughly, going over the predominant emotions she had felt and what they thought the woman could be doing.

'It made me think she was doing a ritual or spell of sorts,' Cassie said. 'It felt like that, with the chanting and movement.'

'Maybe she was,' Sara replied. 'Maybe she was trying to manifest something, a bit like we do today with our intention and gratitude practices.'

'Gratitude practices?' Cassie queried, and Sara went on to explain the process of making our thoughts as positive as possible, by daily listing what we have to be grateful for in our lives, based on the belief that our thoughts create our reality. The more positive we are, the more positive our lives become.

'That's interesting,' Cassie nodded enthusiastically at her mentor and friend. 'Really interesting. Yes, maybe she was doing some manifesting, or magic, whatever you choose to call it. I'm not sure about the figures though, they didn't seem positive to me.'

'No, that was strange,' Sara replied with a quizzical look on her face. 'I'm not sure what they could be but perhaps you could do some research and see what you can find.'

Cassie nodded. 'Her face was interesting though. I'd really like to know what the symbols were about. She'd obviously drawn them on with something, but what they were there for, I have no idea,' and she raised her palm to the ceiling in a gesture of confusion.

'Well, I know a little about symbols,' Sara said, and Cassie leant in slightly, clearly interested in what was to come. 'I know that in healing symbols are keys to different frequencies and that you can use symbols to access those frequencies of energy whenever you need to. I know that they were also used by the ancient tribes as a form of language if you like. So, the Celts created symbols for different trees, which helped them in healing with the benefits of that tree, if that makes sense?' She looked towards Cassie for confirmation.

'So, each symbol created represented a tree, and that symbol was used to help with ailments that the tree helped with?' Cassie repeated.

'Exactly!' Sara said smiling, 'better explained than me.'

Cassie appeared to be deep in thought for a couple of minutes. 'I wonder what these symbols represented then. What energy this woman was trying to access?'

'Maybe more strength to her magic?' Sara suggested.

'Maybe. I'll have to see whether I can draw them in my notebook, although I'm a bit nervous now. Maybe they will initiate something? I could use a bit of magic in my life though,' Cassie smiled wryly.

'Couldn't we all,' Sara replied. 'If you can draw them, you might find them on the internet. They may represent something and give us a bit more information. If this woman is a pagan, they may be calling on the elements of Earth, Air, Fire, and Water?'

'Yes, that's a good idea. I'll have a look and tell you what I find out. The other thing I don't understand,' Cassie continued, 'is the fact that although the figurines were not particularly nice to look at, the whole session didn't make me anxious at all.'

'It might be that you recognised what she was doing on some level, not on a conscious level, but somehow you felt comfortable because it was familiar to you?' Sara suggested and Cassie slowly nodded, clearly unsure about this.

They also discussed how the session could relate to Cassie's current life and whether Cassie knew the woman in this lifetime, but Cassie had not recognised her energy and they both concluded that not all the pieces had yet been revealed, and they would need to keep gathering information in the coming sessions. Cassie felt comforted by her friend's assistance and expertise. At least she was doing something proactive and that feeling helped to spur her on, as did the overwhelming feeling of calm that had washed over her at the end of the session. It had felt so reassuring, and it was a feeling that had not risen in Cassie for some time. In fact, when Cassie thought about this further, she realised that she had never really felt this calm in her entire life. Throughout her childhood, originally with her single mum, and then in foster homes when her mother's alcoholism became more destructive, Cassie realised that there had always been a level of anxiety in her that no amount of support could diffuse. There had always been that feeling that whenever things were going well, it would just as quickly be taken away from her. Although the last foster home had been secure for several years and had enabled Cassie to gain decent grades and go on to university, there had always been a part of her that was on high alert as to what was going to befall her and cause her difficulties again. Even as her life progressed with a positive career path and loving relationships with friends, Joel and his family, this layer of anxiety had never really gone away, and Cassie realised that with the birth of Xander, she was no longer able to keep it small and pushed to the background. She realised that her experience of motherhood had not been a good one, and that scared her a little. She was determined not to follow her own mother's example, but to provide Xander with a loving secure childhood, and be a mother he could be proud of.

As Cassie arrived home an hour or so later following the session, having picked up Xander from her mother-in-law Sophia, she was anxious to complete another entry in her notebook. She placed Xander in his much-loved baby walker and scattered a few raisins on the tray for him to munch on. As he pushed himself around the expansive wooden floor with excitement, Cassie opened the unicorn notebook to her last entry and, below it, wrote the current date and all the additional information that she was able to recall from the latest session.

She then wrote 'WHO is she?' emphasising the 'who'. Was it someone she knew in this lifetime? Why did the red hair stand out? What was the woman doing? She suspected somehow that this was a ritual or spell casting of some sort as they had discussed, but she really didn't know much about it. She suddenly thought about her university friend Alice who had studied some ancient topic about civilisations. Cassie was never sure what it was about, but a conversation with her old friend might certainly help at this time. Cassie reached for her phone. As she texted Alice to see if she was free to meet up this week for a drink and a chat, Xander began to cry. She placed her phone on the countertop and moved to pick him up.

That night Cassie dreamed vividly. It was as if the session had opened a new pathway, and the information just came pouring out. She could see the woman again, but this time she was in a dark space. Cassie couldn't really make out where it was, but the floor seemed to be made of rock and there was water running across it, so she concluded that it was outside somewhere. The woman stood with one foot on either side of a stream, her naked body somehow illuminated, her red hair hanging down her back. This time her hair was tangled, and it looked dirty and unbrushed. Cassie wasn't sure whether this was relevant but noted it even in her dream. The woman's arms were raised high above her head, in a giant V, her face also raised to the light that poured down surrounding her, forming a solid white pillar. The dream lasted only a few seconds, coming in and out of focus, as if her subconscious was just drip-feeding her a bit at a time so as not to overwhelm her. When she thought about it later, Cassie realised that she was excited at what she had seen, as if she was meeting an old friend. This puzzled her.

Over the coming weeks, this scene repeated itself over and over. Sometimes that would be all that Cassie dreamt, other nights her dreams would be so vivid that she would forget the flickering scene amid the other information that poured through. After one particularly vivid night, when she felt as if she could almost smell the moss on the rocks and the cool air of the cave that the woman stood in, Cassie added what information she could recall to the unicorn journal. This time the condition of the woman's hair warranted a new section. Why did it appear unkempt this time? Was something happening to the woman in her life at that moment? Did it represent something or nothing at all? Cassie thought it might be relevant to what was happening to her, and whether she received the information through a session with Sara, or through her dreams, it was part of the puzzle.

The office event had been arranged by Joel's boss as a thank-you for his team, and much to Joel's surprise, Cassie had cheerfully agreed to attend following her resolution to be upbeat and to take more notice of her husband and his world. Joel had been surprised by her keenness for the office get-together which she had blatantly avoided in the past at all costs. He pretended to be pleased but secretly he was also slightly unnerved as he knew that Ava would be there, and he was fearful that Cassie would be able to tell that there was something significant between them. He was so nervous about the impending encounter that he tried several times to talk Cassie out of going. Cassie was equally surprised by her husband's response, having tried to persuade her to attend his office events on numerous occasions, and only saw this as a form of rejection. Cassie believed that her husband was ashamed of her and how she now looked. She felt as if he did not want her by his side and certainly wasn't proud to be seen with her.

The resulting argument caused a cloud of tension to surround them as they silently sat side by side in the car on the journey to the event a few evenings later. They had dropped sleeping Xander off with Joel's mother, together with a paraphernalia of equipment and bags, and had promised to be home in a couple of hours. Cassie felt exhausted even on the run-up to leaving the house. Getting herself ready, Xander fed and ready for bed, and then everything that needed to be packed just in case, had completely worn her out. She felt weary and uncomfortable.

The silence between Cassie and Joel was heavy and a knot of worry wound itself tightly in both their stomachs for different reasons. As the couple walked into the large hotel conference room towards the bank of figures standing around the buffet table, they were silent and not touching. There may as well have been several lifetimes between them.

On the sound of her name, Ava spun around to face them, her long red hair forming a circle around her, swinging almost in slow motion as it spun to slowly catch up with her body. Cassie felt herself start and was conscious that she was trying to keep her face still and without emotion. She did not want this woman to see that she was unnerved, but she was. The hair colour was the same as the woman in the past life. The same wavy copper tresses she had seen in her vision were highlighted now by the overhead lights, which seemed to mock her with their redness. Cassie vaguely recognised Ava, she had seen her before, but only at a distance, at these work events and she realised that the colour of her hair had caused a ripple in her conscious mind during the session. Yet at the time she had not been able to tie down that connection which now suddenly came into sharp definition. Cassie felt an overwhelming sense of foreboding, as if she was so small and vulnerable in the face of this web of scenes and events which the Universe was throwing at her, and which she just didn't understand. She felt lost and frightened standing in front of this unseen force. Why was this happening to her and what did it mean? Even if this woman did have the same hair colour, she certainly didn't have the same face or, indeed, energy. And if she was the same woman, what did it have to do with her and her life? Cassie tried to reason with herself that it was only her imagination, a silly coincidence, but she knew to the core of her being that it was not and that this was a significant piece of information. She knew that the Universe was giving her a clue, but she had no idea what it meant or what she was supposed to do with it.

The rest of the evening was a bit of a blur, the usual platitudes, listening to people's lives who she did not know very well, if at all, and in whom she was not really interested. It just seemed so pointless, and Cassie began to feel grumpy about having to waste her time in this way. The only thing that entertained her was Ava and the colour of her hair. She found herself constantly looking for that copper hue from wherever she was. It was as if Ava the person became unimportant. Her beautiful hair became an entity of its own, the colour taking on a foreboding force and warning like a beacon going off in the room that no one else could see or understand. Cassie did not understand it either, but she was very aware of its presence all night. By the time the evening had drawn to a natural conclusion, Cassie felt emotionally drained from all the unanswered questions whirling around her brain. She was glad to retreat to the comfort and safety of her own life, her child, her husband, and her home. It may not be perfect, but she understood it and knew where she fit within it.

Joel also felt exhausted, but for him, it was through pure tension. He had been coiled tightly all evening watching Cassie watch Ava from wherever they moved in the room. His imagination went into overdrive as he realised that she obviously knew about them. She had not taken her eyes off Ava, her expression puzzled and her demeanour dark. Joel brushed a few beads of sweat off his brow with his handkerchief and tried to stop the panic rising through him. He felt sick with the whole scenario. Maybe he just had to get rid of Cassie. The sudden thought sprung into his head from nowhere and surprised and scared him to his core. He felt a flash of real fear. He didn't know where it had come from. It just seemed to whisper in his mind repeatedly, and he shook his head in an effort to dislodge it. He could see his future descending into a spiral of destruction and unhappiness, yet somehow it also felt familiar and was calling him in a very seductive tone. The fact that he felt drawn to take this path puzzled and frightened him all at the same time.

The evening was not a success for either Cassie or Joel and over the next couple of days the effects troubled them both for different reasons. Joel just couldn't get the destructive thought out of his head no matter how hard he tried to dislodge it, even Ava was not quite enough of a distraction, but he learnt ways to hold it at bay. It greatly unnerved him, and he just wanted to enjoy his mistress and his life. His anger towards Cassie seemed to grow for no reason, other than she was the source of this repeating thought, and therefore it was clearly her fault.

Joel found himself avoiding Cassie as much as possible. He knew at some level it was destructive to their relationship but seeing and speaking to her brought menacing thoughts that he didn't want to have and didn't understand where they were coming from. Joel did his best to try and distract himself, but he just couldn't seem to release himself from the spiral of descent.

He sought out his father one evening after work. He had always been there for him and he knew he would understand. 'Hi, Dad. How are you?' Joel asked as he pushed open the shed door with his elbow, a bottle of opened beer in each hand.

Patrick looked up from his diligent painting of a tiny little soldier that he had secured by one foot in a vice attached to the table in front of him. Attached to a headband was a small torch, brightly illuminating the tiny parts of the figure.

'Joel!' he said, surprise in his voice. 'I didn't know you were coming round. It's lovely to see you, of course,' and he got up from his chair to give his son a hug, putting down his paintbrush as he did so.

'Good to see you too, Dad,' Joel said passing him one of the beer bottles, and wiggling the light around his father's head in fun once he had a free hand. 'Nice torch,' he smiled, but there was no real humour in it. Joel stepped back from the embrace, frightened that it would bring on the tears he could feel welling up and pretended to carefully examine one corner of the model in front of him.

Patrick took in his son's demeanour and took a swig of beer and his seat in almost one motion. 'To what do I owe this pleasure?' he asked, turning off his head torch and looking Joel fully in the eyes, seeing both stress and anxiety. What's this about? he thought to himself, a slight nervous flutter making itself known in his stomach.

Joel dropped his head, knowing that his father was aware of his problem, and had just been waiting for him to reach out. 'I think I need some more help,' he said and then proceeded to tell his father all about the angry emotions that he just couldn't seem to shake.

Patrick was similarly shaken and a little alarmed by his son's confusion. He mused for some time over whether to tell his wife or to keep it to himself. He knew Sophia would be furious if he didn't tell her, so decided on a full and frank discussion. But every time he tried to do so, his nerve would leave him, and the conversation would move on to other things. Instead, he decided to keep it to himself and offered to accompany Joel to some deeper counselling. Patrick was an incredibly organised and efficient man when needed, and this was one of those times. He could always be depended on not to panic in any situation, and to keep his cool. So, swinging into action, over the next few days he not only found a therapist but also booked the sessions and vowed to accompany his son to every appointment.

Patrick was determined that his son's life was not going to unravel and would have done anything to help him heal so that Cassie and Xander stayed in their lives. He was incredibly fond of both his daughter-in-law and his grandson and wanted to see them both grow and blossom during his lifetime. He believed that Joel and Cassie were a good match and didn't want to see the years of history together just thrown away. Sometimes relationships were hard, but it was always worth putting in the effort and trying to make things work for the benefit of all the parties involved.

Patrick and Sophia had worked hard at their relationship over the years, being very different characters, and often reacting in very different ways. When they were newly married, they didn't always understand why the other behaved as they did, but they had worked through it, and now virtually knew what the other was thinking before they did. Their differences had become their strength, either being perfect for different situations and challenges. As soon as Patrick and Sophia had identified this superpower of theirs, there had been no stopping them, and the years had passed in a happy blur. Patrick wanted the same for his only son and was prepared to help him work for it as well.

Joel was less keen on his father's lectures to and from the therapy sessions, however, he acknowledged the fact that his father must know more about a happy marriage than he did, and so – albeit reluctantly at times – he listened to the stories and advice with an open heart and mind. Although he was bored and irritated at times by his father's actions, he was also fully aware of how much he loved him, and he felt very supported and cocooned by his father's love.

Cassie, on the other hand, was still troubled by Ava's hair. She would see it wherever she went. She had never noticed so many redheads before, but now they seemed to be everywhere, and she was acutely aware of them. Cassie had no problem with redheads, in fact, she loved the colour and had been a dyed redhead herself on many occasions over the years. She loved the warmth of the colour and how it made her skin look, and the contrast with her hazel eyes. But now redheads seemed to taunt her subconscious, teasing her with some information that Cassie couldn't quite understand. It left her feeling exhausted and tense. What did all this mean? In desperation, she telephoned Sara in the hope that a chat with her friend could help her. Of course, there were no instant answers which just made Cassie even more frustrated.

'What do you think it means?' she asked Sara. 'I've racked my brain for some sort of answer, but it just feels so elusive. As if it's just out of reach.'

'You're never going to understand it unless you give yourself some headspace. Why don't you come over for a Reiki treatment? It will help you relax about everything. The tenser you are, the less likely that any answers are going to come to you,' Sara concluded.

'I know you're right,' Cassie said, sighing deeply. 'I just feel so muddled and uncertain about everything. I know I must just go with the flow, but it's so difficult.'

'I know it is but there's a reason why this is happening, and I believe that the answers will literally be life-changing for you. You just need to be patient.'

Cassie laughed, 'I know,' she squealed, 'but it's so frustrating!'

Sara laughed too. 'Okay, you are definitely coming over for a Reiki treatment. You need to relax. Let's say Friday at 4 p.m., and I won't take no for an answer.'

Hinat

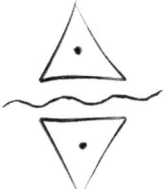

Hinat strolled down the narrow street, her long blue dress quickly becoming streaked around the hem with the characteristic red dust of the region. Her beautiful copper tresses were held back from her face with a white woven scarf, carefully wrapped around her head, protecting her scalp, forehead, and ears from the intense heat of the sun. She carried a reed basket over her arm. Around her waist was a rope belt which looped her slim body twice, and attached to this was a purse holding the few coins she needed to get some supplies.

Hinat's tall stance was youthful and straight, her walk energised. She was a striking woman, and many turned to look at her as she strolled past. Their expressions were often ones of awe and smiles would cross their faces as they watched her pass. Hinat was used to this response from others and would often smile back, amused at their reactions. Hinat stood out not only for her striking stature but also for her energy, which was powerful and palpable. Just being in her presence, even for a moment, could positively affect those around her.

Hinat loved her hometown of Raqmu, her life there, the people and even the red dust which eventually permeated everything. She loved the smells of the place which were so familiar to her, and which she had known since her childhood. Everywhere you walked the aroma of frankincense – commonly used in the temples and often mixed with other scents such as myrrh, elemi, and the local iris – was evident. People would also sprinkle their clothes with the contents of the little pottery perfume bottles (made and sold all over Raqmu) as part of their daily ablutions. This created different aromas floating in the air, several of which Hinat caught today as she walked briskly on.

Hinat had been born to a long-established nomadic family, her ancestors selling frankincense, myrrh and the much sought-after tinctures from the beautiful iris of the region, along the area's spice trails for as long as they could remember. Hinat loved the local flora that would burst suddenly into life after the rains had been and used them constantly in her work. She loved the colours and the scents of the flowers and plants, and how the tinctures and poultices she made could help a variety of ailments. Her favourite was the beautiful Iris of Raqmu, with its dark sultry colour which matched the rocks of the region, and which brought such relief to her clients.

After many years of nomadic life, her father had decided to break tradition and find more stability for his family. He had brought them to settle in Raqmu, where he believed they would be accepted. He was right. Hinat's father was a priest, involved in the burial cities which served the wealthiest Nabataeans throughout the region. Raqmu was known as the inner kingdom, and its burial tombs were the largest of all the burial cities. Her father had trained her not only in the physical preparation of the dead but in the ceremonies designed to help the souls of the departed to move on to a different dimension too. Raqmu was full of the departed, carefully laid to rest in one of the one hundred or so huge tombs, built majestically into and from the red rock of the region. Huge doorways marked the entrances, often with the common crowstep symbol adorning the archways. Her brothers had trained as sculptors, to assist with the building of these tombs, which they believed would number around one thousand if their plans were eventually fully realised.

Positioned around the tombs were an array of stone houses built into the rock as well. These were for the priests, those who served the royal courts and public buildings, as well as the sculptors, gravediggers, and other administrative staff who were needed to run and organise the city. Even further out from the centre were huge settlements of nomadic tents, around which were the dug graveyards for the rest of the population. Nabateans who died whilst away from the city would often be given an air burial where they died, carefully laid out to the vultures and the elements. Once they were just bones, they would be collected and brought back to the temples of Raqmu. It might have seemed barbaric to others, but it was important that their bones were cleaned and reclaimed, to be placed within their community. In the temples of Raqmu, the remains would be blessed and anointed and placed in a jar to be buried alongside others within the tombs. It was tradition that their physical remnants were laid to rest in this beautiful burial city, and their souls were guided by the priests and priestesses.

Such bone retrievals were part of Hinat's work, and collecting the bones of the dead from the many high-exposure platforms that surrounded the outer limits of the city was a regular task for her. Whilst there she would top up the small pottery bottles of patchouli placed carefully around the platforms and burn her beloved frankincense resin in small pottery bowls. She would also lay out plates of fruit grown in the region, such as apricots, peaches, and figs. These would quickly soften and decay in the heat of the sun, but they created sugar-filled food for the bees, her little helpers. Bees were an important part of the region, creating beautiful honey in the makeshift hives built all around the city: large spherical shapes of straw and wet clay, with a top lid for easy collection of the honey and wax, and a small hole at the base allowing the bees to come and go. The large numbers of them were familiar sights all around the high cliffs and crevices of the city. The bees were also important in Hinat's work with the dead, as they could move across the veil, living in both worlds and bringing her messages from beyond. They would often pass information to her as she busied around the air burial sites, and she communed with them happily. As the scents of the incense hung in the air, and the bees buzzed around her, Hinat would sit quietly, chanting and humming, the sounds being as important as the smells in clearing the space of any negative energy that may be lingering there, waiting to steal the bones or block the passage of the souls.

Hinat swiftly made her way to the upper marketplace today. She needed to buy supplies for her temple and was always excited to go to the market. There were three marketplaces in Raqmu – lower, middle, and upper – but the upper was where Hinat knew she would be able to buy the oils, crystals, and pottery items that she needed. The upper marketplace was assigned to the temple work and was always full of beautiful frankincense resin, pottery and metal bowls for ceremonial purposes, spices, herbs, oils, crystals, feathers, shells, and all sorts of temple items. A lot of the items were not from the region but were brought in with the nomadic tribes that still traded as far as the Mediterranean. There were also beautiful scarves, dresses and coats for the priest and priestesses to choose from, each temple having a specific colour theme. Hinat and her father's temple workers always wore blue, adorning themselves with different shades of blue clothing and jewellery and picking mainly blue crystals to work with. Theirs was the temple where communication, song and sound were celebrated, the blue activating the throat and face chakras of both the workers and the dead. Those who were particularly good at singing would gravitate to the temple, but humming and chanting were just as important.

Hinat had studied hard with her father, very conscious of the shift that their choice had made to the ancestral line, and aware that they needed to be successful for that very reason. Hinat's father was a compassionate and kind man, but also a shrewd one, and he had deliberately encouraged Hinat to train as a priestess, as well as engaging his three sons to gain apprenticeships as sculptors, knowing that there would be years of work for them and that they would acquire a permanent stone residence to live in. Eventually, Hinat would also acquire a stone house of her own. She did not need to marry to do so but needed to complete her apprenticeship first. The Nabateans celebrated their women, who were not only equal to the men but were also often celebrated for their powerful female virtues. Hinat felt extremely blessed to be born into such a tribe, where she was not only equal to her brothers but could succeed them with hard work and some luck on her side.

The stone homes that her family had been able to own were more prestigious than the nomadic tents of their ancestors, although Hinat had always thought the tents of her early childhood romantic and extremely comfortable. However, she had to admit that the stone homes were warmer in the colder months from December to February, and cooler in the intense heat of the summer. They were also riddled with caves and passages leading far back into the rock structures, which if you were lucky, created additional cool spaces where provisions would last much longer, as well as safe areas for treasures to be hidden in the nooks and crannies.

Hinat's father had a large stone home, with whom Hinat lived as his only daughter, together with a housemaid to help them with the usual chores while they were both busy with their temple work. Hinat's mother had passed when Hinat was still a baby, having contracted an infection shortly after her birth, and Hinat had no real memory of her. Her three older brothers had their own homes with their wives, children, and housemaids, which Hinat knew was a matter of pride for her father and their ancestors.

This morning, Hinat spent a couple of relaxed and enjoyable hours collecting the provisions that she needed. She loved losing herself between the market stalls, allowing her mind to focus only on the beautiful items in front of her, whilst searching through all the wares for something slightly different. It was almost like a meditation for her. She would usually recognise other priests and priestesses who were there for the same reason and would enjoy chatting to them, as well as the various traders whom she had come to know well over time. She adored her work with the dead and had a passion for the crystals and rocks of the region. She would create grids and piles of them in her temple, arranged in geometric swirls and patterns, intuitively knowing that this was important. It was something unique to her work and her father fully encouraged her different ideas if it created a reverent and sacred space for the work that they did. Often Hinat would also place crystals within the jars of bones, or in the small crevices or spaces where the bones were laid. She would take great care to arrange them carefully and with the utmost respect. Sometimes slightly larger spaces which contained full bodies or skeletons would have stone shelves or crevices running at different heights, carved, and shaped into the walls, and Hinat would arrange the jars and crystals in groups and patterns along the thin ledges. When there was more space, she would also add little pottery bottles of incense or oil, small pottery lamps, and bowls and coins depicting the Gods and Goddesses. She knew that all the souls connected to these bones would eventually find each other on the other side, living together in their community across the veil forever. Hinat was aware that the crystals cleared the energy of the space and smoothed the way for the souls to pass as they travelled. She had also come to realise that the crystals could be used to store information. Each crystal contained information about each of the souls, which they could take with them. Information regarding their ancestors, their lives and whether they had succeeded in what they had come to do in this lifetime. The bees would also take messages across the veil, to be compiled in records for all time on all the souls that had ever been born and died. It was important for the souls to be in social groups as they traversed, so much so that a lot of the sculptors had started creating dining rooms, courtyards, gardens, and other spaces so that the dead could initially socialise, before moving on to review their lives and what they had, and in some cases had not, achieved. Hinat would also ensure that these spaces and rooms were laid out with furniture and decorated with crystals, perfumes, and little pottery statues so that the souls would be happy and joyous once together again.

All the temple workers had great pride in their work, understanding that they were working with the energetic souls of the departed, and creating a path for them to follow to be with the Gods. They also believed that to show disrespect for their work would bring the wrath of the Gods and Goddesses down on their heads. Hinat was different though. She was full of respect for the work that she did, and she loved working with the Gods' and Goddesses' energies, but she was also aware that there was an overall energy. 'Spirit' as she called it, was all around them, permeating every part of the beautiful city, and every part of her. She knew that Spirit was able to talk to her and help her with her life. Hinat would often know things, or hear words whispered in her ear when no physical body was there, and she knew that Spirit was assisting her. It made perfect sense to her that as she was helping the dead to depart, they in turn would also help her from the other side, and she would often see their spirits smiling and waving to her as she went about her work. In fact, the temples were always full of spirits mingling around and Hinat had been surprised to discover that the other temple workers could not see them as she could. She did not always let them know what she could see, as she didn't want to stand out, but she was often aware of the workers' energies as well. Hinat would see their energy bubbles in different colours and any disturbances or issues that were stopping the energy flowing as it should, would be highlighted for her. If she watched them long enough, she would get visual flashes in her third eye of their life, giving her valuable information about them, and the probable cause of any disturbance. She would also feel the energy streaming through her own hands at this time and would direct that energy with her intention and thought to the problem area, watching as the energies merged and swirled together, eventually distributing and settling the upset. It was something that she had always been able to do and others would often come to her for a healing. She enjoyed helping the other temple workers in this way, making sure everyone was happy and working well.

Twice a year, Hinat, her father and all the temple staff would be run off their feet, organising the festivals for the dead, where families and relatives would come to remember their departed. Huge tables would be set out with cheap crockery for the relatives to celebrate, drinking and eating well into the night. It was a busy time for them all and Hinat would often get all the workers together early to give them a group healing, topping up their energies and revitalising them for the day ahead. Once the guests had finished eating and drinking, the cutlery and crockery would be broken and smashed as was the tradition. The piles of broken pieces would need to be collected by the temple staff, washed carefully, and stored in hessian bags for later use by the temples in creating mosaic floors and artwork. Nothing was wasted. It was hard work and required much organisation but Hinat did it willingly, knowing that it was an important part of the grieving process for those left behind. Of course, once it was over, they were all relieved from the days of planning and preparation, and her father would kindly allow them a day off to sleep, recharge and recover. Hinat always loved those days. It meant that she could catch up on her sleep, bathe and meditate, and chat to her beloved Spirit in more depth. The way that she now heard Spirit had developed over the years and was as clear as chatting to a friend. Hinat would ensure that she was washed and anointed before commencing her conversations, showing huge respect for this powerful and unseen force.

As Hinat made her way carefully down the steps to the temple, her basket was overflowing and she excitedly went to find her father to show him her purchases. Once her father had seen and approved of his beloved daughter's new items, he sent her off to check the symbols that were adorned on various walls of the temples and the surrounding rocks. These symbols were hugely important to show respect for the Gods, to ward off any evil spirits and to protect their temple space. Hinat always felt that the symbols vibrated, and she carefully traced their shapes across the rock, using dark red paste made by mixing the local soil with fragrant oil. She could feel and hear the vibrations that they gave off and would often try and match it with her voice, creating chants and sounds as she worked. It was a heady mixture of smell, vibration, and sound and Hinat knew that it was a powerful and protective tool. Often other workers would come to her, frightened of retaliation from a relative or from their Gods for something they had done, begging for a protective symbol from Hinat. She would talk to them about their behaviour and how it would probably be better to communicate with the other party and offer their apologies, but she would always send them off with a personal symbol etched on their palms or arms to protect them from any trouble or ongoing bad feeling. She had gained quite a reputation for this.

During the afternoon of her market visit, one of the priestesses of another temple came to find her. 'Hello Hinat. How are you?' Gamilat said. She was a tall, pretty girl. Her long dark hair was shiny and tied back in a ponytail, and her deep purple dress skimmed her slim body revealing gentle curves. Gamilat's temple wore purple and celebrated sight of all types, whether by the eyes or the mind.

'Hello Gamilat, I'm good thank you,' Hinat responded smiling at her good friend.

'I wanted to talk to you,' Gamilat whispered.

Hinat nodded at her and motioned to the stone steps behind them, walking in front of her friend to sit on the top one. Gamilat sat beside her and Hinat took her hand – seeing that Gamilat was clearly concerned about something. 'What's going on?' she asked Gamilat, peering into her face as she said it. 'You look upset.'

Gamilat sighed and her voice shook as she spoke, her eyes filling slightly with tears. 'It's my husband. I know he's seeing our housemaid. I've seen it in the pools. They are always giggling together and I just find it disrespectful. We haven't been married that long. How could he behave like this?' Her voice found its strength again as anger flooded to the fore.

'Really? Why indeed?' Hinat commented, also feeling angry at this behaviour. How could he be so stupid she thought silently. Gamilat had the sight herself and could see everything that was going on, often scrying in the small man-made reservoirs that surrounded her temple. 'How can I help?' she asked, emphasising the I.

'Well, I was hoping that you could give me a symbol or a spell to make her dislike him?'

Hinat looked a little startled at this. It was not something that she had ever done before. 'I'm not sure how to do that,' Hinat confessed. 'I can give you a symbol for protection, but to stop the affections of someone is slightly different,' she said, her brows knitting as the thoughts immediately started whirring in her head.

'I know it's not your usual thing, but I wondered if you would give it some thought and see what you come up with,' Gamilat asked, her pleading eyes huge and moist. 'I saw you in the pools doing something very similar for others. It's your path Hinat and you might as well start with me.'

'Really! Well, if you say so.' Hinat smiled at the priestess, squeezing her hand for reassurance. 'I'll meditate on it and see what I come up with.'

'Oh, thank you Hinat, you're amazing!' Gamilat wrapped her arms around Hinat's shoulders, giving her an appreciative hug. Hinat patted her arm. She felt a little less sure than her friend but knew that she would give it her full attention.

Over the coming weeks, Gamilat's words reverberated in Hinat's head and she began to feel excited. Was she really going to make spells? Her ancestors had been apt at spells and potions, and she had heard stories of the process and results. It was not something she had thought about for herself, but Gamilat had seen it in the pools, so it was a possibility. Hinat vowed to get away as soon as possible to meditate on a solution for her friend.

That time didn't materialise for a few days but one afternoon her father announced that she could go early as the temple was looking organised and all the chores had been completed. Hinat gratefully kissed him on the cheek and rushed home as fast as she could. Hagru, their maid, was out and Hinat knew this was the time she had been waiting for. She washed and changed her clothes, then entering her own room, and ensuring that the door was closed behind her, she set her intention to speak to Spirit and find a solution to Gamilat's problem. She methodically made a circle of her favourite crystals – used specifically for meditation. She interspersed them with tiny pottery lamps into which she poured oil and carefully inserted wicks, which she then lit. As the light from the lamps joined in a circle of light, the crystals twinkled and glistened. Hinat lit some frankincense resin in a small pottery bowl and laid it to one side, allowing the familiar aroma to waft across the circle and around her room. She wrapped a red sheer scarf around her head in reverence to Spirit and sat cross-legged in the middle of the circle. The red of the scarf and the copper of her hair clashed slightly, but Hinat was of no mind. She loved the similarity and clashing of the colours, it made her feel alive, and pinning the scarf to one side, she closed her eyes and allowed her mind to slow down and settle, as she sank into a deep state of relaxation.

It was as if her mind slowed to almost a standstill, and then suddenly she could step into a circle of light and movement again, mirroring the shape and size of the circle in her physical room. It was from this space that she could commune with Spirit and gain huge insight into any situation that was troubling her. Today it was Gamilat's problem, and she gently asked what she could do to help. The response was immediate – Hinat did not hear it as words this time but as visions in her mind's eye. She could see the housemaid not just as a physical being but as an energetic entity, her energy like a bright, colourful bubble around her. She could see the bubble being bound as if with a giant scarf, obscuring the housemaid from view. The image faded as quickly as it had come and Hinat continued, asking other questions, and obtaining further answers as to how this could be achieved.

Later, once she had fully come back to the present, she contemplated the information she had been given. The housemaid's energy could be bound so that she would no longer be seen by the husband on an energetic level, and he would lose interest. To do that Hinat needed to create a physical representative of the housemaid and give it to Gamilat to burn. What that physical image should be she was not sure, but according to Spirit it really didn't matter. It simply represented the housemaid's energy. Hinat mulled over this as she busied herself with a few household chores and prepared a light supper for herself. She eventually decided that whatever she used needed to look sufficiently restricting if others were going to understand its purpose, and an image eventually came to her. She decided to try to use the wax collected from the beehives to mould the image she had seen. That way Gamilat could burn it and initiate the spell.

Hinat hunted through her belongings, which were piled in two large baskets to one side of her bed, until she found the little wooden box she had been looking for. Inside it were old beeswax candle stumps which she had collected from the temple after the latest ceremonies. Wax was in great supply from the region's bees, although oil and wicks were preferred by some temples, but Hinat always collected the stumps of the used candles when she could, knowing that they would come in handy in the future. The beehives of the region were also able to produce pollen, royal jelly, and bee venom, which she knew could be of assistance in very small doses. She fished out the cleanest wax chunks, scrapping all the usable wax from the long wicks, and arranged it in the pottery bowl that she often used for incense. Placing the bowl on the floor, she carefully moved the flame of the lighted lamp around the edge, creating enough heat for the wax to start to melt. Continuing until the wax was malleable, she then carefully eased out a chunk, testing the temperature as she went. Finding the point where she didn't burn her hands but the wax was usable, was difficult and took a few attempts, but eventually, and working very quickly, she was able to mould the wax into a figure. With the heat of her hands, the wax continued to be workable until eventually, she could no longer alter it. Hinat worked for a while, pulling, and probing the wax until she placed the resulting figure on the ground in front of her. It was a figure of a woman kneeling, with her hands and feet tied behind her. Hinat studied her work and was pleased with what she saw, although she wondered if it would look frightening to some people. She shook her head. It had to be obvious to everyone what it was being used for, for the intention to be strong. She worked on the housemaid's energy a little more, as that was how she saw it, and when she closed her eyes and saw the housemaid in her mind's eye, she could see the outer edge of her energy bubble becoming opaque until she was no longer visible.

Once finished, Hinat placed the little figure carefully in the middle of a hessian square that she had retrieved from her baskets, wrapping the four corners around the figure, turning it over to hold them secure, and then encircling it with some twine. She held the package up by the string, so that it dangled in front of her, and smiled triumphantly. She had done it! She had created a binding spell doll for Gamilat. She was so excited and very eager to see how well it worked. Hinat had no doubt that it would, after all, Spirit had advised her on this, but she was keen to see how quickly the relationship died. As an afterthought, Hinat rubbed her finger in some of the residue from one of her lamps and etched a protective symbol on the edge of the cloth, ensuring that only the person for whom the spell was meant would be affected. She then carefully placed the little package in her basket to take with her to the temple the next morning. It was now late, and Hinat hurried to get ready for bed knowing that she had a lot of temple chores to get through the next day. As she drifted off to sleep, she smiled at her accomplishment and thanked Spirit for the help and guidance she had received.

Hinat rose early the next morning after a deep relaxing sleep. Even though she had gone to sleep later than usual because of the spell-making, she had slept well and felt energised. She walked quickly to the temple, bringing some breakfast for her and her father to share. Her father had been busy all night with blessings and ceremonies and when she arrived at the temple he was changing from his robes. He gave her a big grin. 'Good morning daughter. How are you today?'

'Good thank you, Father. I've brought us breakfast,' and she started placing the food on the table, as he came to sit with her.

'Excellent, thank you.'

'How was last night? Did you get through everything you wanted to?'

Her father smiled wearily. 'I did. It's so much quieter at night, so peaceful, and I can get through so many blessings for people, but it does wear me out.'

'You need to go home and rest now,' Hinat instructed him. 'I don't want you getting ill. Hagru will be there later but she won't disturb you. Go and get some sleep.' She patted his shoulder for emphasis.

'I will, I will.' Strabo looked at his only daughter, his eyes soft and a faint smile on his face. He was so proud of the woman she had become, of her kindness and compassion which he saw all the time with the way she treated Hagru and the temple workers. She was a lovely person and his heart swelled with pride. Strabo was also very aware that she was incredibly strong energetically, and that she would surpass his capabilities in the temple easily. Again, a wave of pride washed over him. Of all his children he knew that his daughter had an amazing connection with Spirit and would be celebrated for that.

Once they had eaten, Strabo wearily stood up, leaning on the table to help him. Hinat rushed to get his coat and helped him put it on, before kissing his cheek and watching him leave the temple, heading home to bed. She shook her head slightly as she watched him go, relieved that he would be getting some rest, but concerned that he seemed so tired these days.

Hinat continued her work at the temple that day, fully present in her tasks and assisting the other workers when they needed it. Eventually, everyone left to go to their own homes, except Aretas and Rabble who helped her pull the giant wooden doors to the temple shut and secure them for the night. The doors to the temple were heavy and Hinat needed assistance to shut them on the evenings that her father did not stay. Of course, they did not worry about anyone coming into the temple and doing harm, as the population had a healthy fear of the wrath of the Gods and Goddesses should they misbehave, but they preferred to close them and not provide any temptation. The doors would also protect the temple from the dust storms that sometimes whipped up during the night. Hinat thanked the two men for their assistance and watched them walk away, home to their own families, as she dawdled on the steps waiting for Gamilat. It wasn't long before she appeared, a broad smile across her face as she welcomed Hinat.

'You look happy,' Hinat said. 'Do you still need this spell?' and she dangled the little package in front of Gamilat's face.

Gamilat's eyes widened and she smiled again. 'Of course. I'm just not going to allow him to make me unhappy. I'm not allowing it to intrude my thoughts all day, every day. I don't want to get into a state about it, so I'm trying to keep positive.'

'Good for you,' Hinat replied. 'That's a healthy way to be. Here you go then, take it and I hope that it helps the situation.'

'Oh, I have no doubt,' and Gamilat tucked the little package in her basket, gave Hinat a coin out of her pocket, and almost skipped down the steps.

Hinat looked down at the very generous coin in her palm and smiled. There was something really satisfying about earning money from a task that you loved.

A few days later Gamilat reported that her husband had got bored with the housemaid, and she had gone to work for another family, upset that she was no longer seen by her lover. Gamilat was ecstatic and word quickly spread as to how Hinat had helped her.

Hinat swiftly gained a reputation for her work. She was regularly visited by clients requesting spell dolls, as well as tablets which she later added. Hinat loved the work, knowing that she was helping others, and enjoying the connection and assistance from Spirit, but also loving the creative side of the work. She would add spices and herbs if they were relevant, flowers, leaves or roots, even fish bones she collected from the banquets when fish had been brought up from the Mediterranean for the feasts, and of course the bee venom in small doses that would cause irritation in its recipients. She would also add shell fragments sometimes, which a trader had given her for free as he was unable to sell the broken pieces, for a similar purpose. There was really no end to her creative ideas and the success of her spells grew steadily. Hinat also used the ideas to add potions and concoctions to the temple, scattering different plants and herbs to help the spirits in some way. Their temple was praised for their innovative ways and this was another moment of pride for Strabo.

Strabo knew he was dying. He had his own connection with Spirit. He had taught his daughter from infancy how to connect and converse with this power, as he had learnt from his father, and so on down the generations. He had seen his death in a vision but it didn't frighten him. In a way, he was looking forward to crossing over to the realms of Spirit. His body ached and he was in constant pain with his lower back. He had noticed a strange taste to all his food of late and knew that he had lost weight because of it. He was also aware that there was a mass in his stomach and that his time was now fast approaching.

Strabo had sought out some herbal medicine to assist him and he took it regularly, but he could tell that it was not as effective as it had been initially. The disease was progressing and some days he struggled to get to the temple at all. He knew that he would need to explain to Hinat what was happening, but his heart ached at the idea of that meeting. He decided to get all his children together to tell them of his condition and arranged a dinner for them all. Hagru was not impressed with this sudden request, but when he quietly explained to her the reason and to keep it to herself for now, her eyes filled with tears, and she threw her heart and soul into the preparations. Hinat was surprised that her three brothers were all coming to dinner. Including their wives, there would be eight of them and she went to the kitchen to help Hagru with the preparations. However, Hagru was having none of it and told her to enjoy her family, and that she could cope with everything. That's not like Hagru, Hinat thought, but decided to do as she was told. It wasn't often they were all together, and she loved the banter and teasing that inevitably went on. They enjoyed the dinner that was put in front of them and then Strabo banged on the table for silence.

'Thank you all for coming over tonight. It's been lovely to

have you all here again and to see that you are all happy and well. I am proud of everything you have all accomplished and I hope that you will continue to support each other when I'm gone.' He looked around at the slightly bemused expressions on his family's faces.

'What are you talking about, Father?' his eldest asked. 'You are going to outlive all of us!' The others laughed and smiled.

'Unfortunately, I'm not. I'm ill and I haven't got much time left.' The laughter and smiles faded rapidly, and Hinat rushed to her father's side.

'Why didn't you tell me?' she pleaded, tears beginning to brim over her eyes.

'Because I didn't want you to worry or be upset,' he patted her arm. 'I'm happy to go. You are all doing well, and I know that my time is coming.' He wrapped his arms around his sobbing daughter's shoulders and gently comforted her. 'It's okay, it's fine. I'm happy to go,' he told her.

Once Strabo had acknowledged the disease to his children, it was as if he could finally relax and let go, and the illness progressed quickly. One evening, surrounded by his children, Strabo took his final breath and stepped over the veil, clutching in his hand a crystal gifted by Hinat, with the wisps of frankincense heavy in the air.

Ava

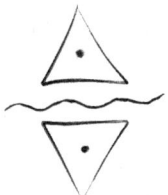

Ava kicked off her scarlet stilettos at the first opportunity upon arriving home. Home was a beautiful apartment with large sash windows overlooking a quiet tree-lined street. The rooms were mainly white with high ceilings, and the furnishings minimal and modern – which created an illusion of space. Ava headed straight to the bedroom which was painted in a dark maroon red. It was a complete contrast to the rest of the flat and Ava loved the feeling of being cocooned in this space, warm and safe. Other than the walls, everything else was white or crystal, allowing ribbons of multi-coloured light to bounce around and break up any feelings of heaviness.

Ava quickly undressed and put on her short pyjamas before diving into bed and enveloping herself in the large soft duvet. She was tired from the evening but sleep did not come easily and she tossed and turned as the events of the night played through her mind like a constant stream of images.

Cassie's eyes had followed her all evening. Wherever she was in the room she had sensed someone looking at her and knew that it was Joel's wife. She had avoided turning around each time but the effort of not doing so went against every instinct. She knew without a shadow of a doubt that Cassie suspected something was happening between them, and she slowly smiled to herself as this realisation took hold and a wave of achievement and excitement flowed through her. Ava felt no fear of discovery, nor shame at her behaviour, just relish at the way she was able to successfully manipulate Joel and his wife, and therefore manifest what she wanted in her life. She did not know how Cassie had found out and she did not care, but it was to her favour and for that she was very grateful to the unseen forces of the Universe.

Ava slowly opened her eyes as she struggled to wake up and lay looking at the ceiling, her attention on the sound of the wood pigeon outside her bedroom window. The seemingly melancholy call of the bird became almost hypnotic as she lay there, allowing it to wash over her, and her mind to wander. The bird's call abruptly came to an end and Ava equally as abruptly came back to the present moment. She pulled herself up slightly in bed, propping an extra pillow under her head, and lay there relishing the chance to just relax. On every normal weekday morning, she would be out of bed at 6 a.m., getting dressed and prepping for her day's appointments and meetings. On Sundays, like today, she could just lie in bed and give herself some space to think about her life and the elements within it. Ava was not only a very attractive girl but also bright and ambitious. Her beautiful long copper hair contrasted with her pale skin and big grey eyes. Her colouring was not that of a typical redhead; her hair contained a large amount of brown and her complexion, although fair, had more of an olive tone, which tanned relatively well in the sun. The resulting image was both unique and stunning.

As Ava lay wrapped in her white cotton bedding, she gazed around her room taking in the crystal furniture and the carefully placed ornaments. Her apartment was tidy and ordered with everything in its place. She loved this flat, having her own space and being in complete control of it. That for her was a major driving force in her life. She needed to be in control of everything she did. She needed to succeed at any cost and create some security in her life.

Ava had always been ambitious. She came from a family of achievers who pushed themselves relentlessly, and not being successful was not a choice. Her three older brothers had all done well for themselves and had lovely homes and families. Her father was a military man who had been very strict on the only girl in the family, pushing and prodding her so much that at times she would be in tears of frustration. However, any sign of weakness would initiate a torrent of abuse and disgust from her father, and she quickly learned to not cry for any reason and to hide her true emotions. Ava loved her father more than anything and just wanted him to be proud of her but was aware that his parenting skills had not been conventional or kind. This combination of experiences in the way that she had been brought up led her to be cold, manipulative at times, and ruthlessly ambitious. Ava had also discovered that her looks could help her get what she wanted from men, and she had used this to her advantage many times. She had never developed a relationship before based on true affection, but only to progress her career or social standing. In fact, Ava did not believe she had ever been in love and was not sure that she wanted that sort of relationship. She had seen her friends heartbroken and crushed and she knew that she did not want to be on the receiving end of that. What she wanted was to be seen as incredibly successful in her own right as a woman, and with that success would come power. Power at work and power within her own personal life, completely in control and therefore secure. Her father would be proud of her once she had achieved this status and the thought propelled her on relentlessly.

Sometimes her manipulation had not worked in the way that she wanted, but she was never deterred from trying again, picking herself up and moving on to the next relationship or situation. Her inability to feel emotion worried her at times. She knew that she had a wall around her heart but, just like Joel, she was not prepared to delve into the reasons for that wall or to remove it. To her, not being able to be hurt by others was a necessary and effective part of her armour as she pushed on through the battles of life.

Ava's thoughts turned to the office party the night before and to Joel. Instantly, she felt a flutter in her stomach as she pictured him and immediately pushed that away. She did not want to feel too much or to fall in love. That was far too difficult and too frightening to really open herself to the emotions involved. But she did want Joel and she was adamant that she would get him no matter who she hurt on the way. Joel was more experienced at work and led the most successful team in the Company. She knew that if she could also get on that team, she could work her way up, learning on the way and eventually superseding him at the top.

Ava thought about Cassie without much emotion as well. She could see how attractive and what a genuinely nice person she was, but those traits were of no importance to Ava. They did create a barrier to her ambitions, however, and she knew that Cassie could stop her from being with Joel. The thought of the baby also momentarily tugged at her conscience but again she pushed it away, placing it securely in a locked box in her mind somewhere. She was not going to delve into those emotions at all. What she had to do was to focus on what she wanted – and that was Joel. Once he was hooked, she could manoeuvre herself onto his team and then work her way up from there. It would give her a massive boost to her position within the Company, and to her ego. She relived their relationship in her mind and felt a sense of accomplishment and pride. She was also aware that she felt more but was not sure whether that was love or something else.

Ava glanced at the clock to her side and saw that it was nearly ten o'clock. She stumbled out of bed and padded softly to the kitchen to make her usual pot of real coffee. She was such a coffee snob, preferring only the best quality coffee beans which she freshly ground every weekend morning. As she prepared the coffee, she thought about what she was going to do for the rest of the day. Ava, for the most part, enjoyed living on her own, but sometimes weekends felt lonely to her, and she often looked forward to starting early on a Monday morning, just for the company of others and the feeling that she had a purpose. Today, though, she had another plan in mind.

Ava quickly showered and dressed in her sleek jogging attire, placing her phone and house keys into a specially designed pouch on her arm and pushing her earphones into her ears so she had something to listen to or to take telephone calls while she ran. Running was such an escape for Ava, and she loved the way that it not only kept her fit but allowed her mind to wander wherever it needed to go. It helped her to relax and to keep any semblance of anxiety at bay. These were the times when she was most creative, letting her mind just drift, and coming up with amazing plans and ideas.

Today she was thinking about Joel and where their relationship was going, and she had the urge to call him. She didn't usually contact him two days in a row, and in fact, would try not to, but today she really wanted to see him again and find out if anything had been said between him and his wife the night before. She wanted to know whether her presence in his life was making a ripple that others could see. She wanted to know whether she should increase the manipulation and take her plans to the next level.

As she stepped out of her front door, Ava glanced across the road to the sound of the bird cawing so loudly that the sound seemed to physically reverberate through the quiet street. She squinted as she tried to find the source of the noise, before locating a large black bird positioned on a branch on the other side of the road. It was looking directly at her, and Ava suddenly felt uncomfortable. She stood very still but the bird's beady gaze did not falter. Ava moved slowly onto the pavement, never taking her eyes off the bird who continued its strident call and intent stare. She suddenly shook her head as if to break free of the trance she had fallen into, and started chuckling to herself for being so silly, before glancing sideways down the street. She just noticed a cyclist going at speed at the last minute and had to step back suddenly to avoid being hit, muttering a profanity to herself under her breath. He, in turn, swore at her, raising a finger in an aggressive gesture as he flew past. Ava straightened herself and taking a deep breath, quickly crossed the road. She looked for the bird, which should have now been directly above her, but it had gone. As she settled into a gentle jogging rhythm, she pressed the pre-set button on her phone to contact Joel, realising that she was a bit shaken by the cyclist and bird incident. She shook her hands out as she jogged to release any tension, and gratefully listened to the ringing tone with a mixture of excitement and a small amount of apprehension.

Joel was sitting at the kitchen table nursing a slight headache and trying to concentrate on reading the Sunday papers. He had a mug of black coffee in his right hand, which he never put down while deftly turning the pages with his free left hand. He was aware of the sounds of Cassie and Xander as they cleared out one of the kitchen cupboards together in the background, the soft chatter and occasional adorable giggle from his son, but his thoughts were on Ava. He knew that she was slowly getting under his skin. He delighted in that thought but also felt a splinter of fear in his heart. He listened to Xander giggling again, cocking his head slightly to one side and smiling gently at the sound, although his eyes portrayed the conflicting emotions within him. Suddenly, he jumped, spilling his coffee as the mobile next to him rang. He swore as he stood up to avoid the spillage trickling into his lap, and hesitated for a moment as he decided whether or not to put the phone on the loudspeaker facility. He clamped the phone to his ear. 'Hello,' he answered sharply.

'Hi, it's me,' Ava replied. 'Sorry to ring you at home. Can you talk?'

Joel was shocked and slightly annoyed that Ava had rung him at home. Why would she be so reckless? He glanced over to the numerous Tupperware containers sprawled across the kitchen floor and his wife's head just visible over the kitchen counter. He lowered his voice. 'I'm fine for a minute. Why are you ringing me here?'

The annoyance in his voice translated clearly to Ava and she recoiled slightly before allowing her ego to spring back into shape. 'I wanted to talk to you, that's why. I wanted to make sure everything was okay after last night. Cassie obviously suspects something between us, she never took her eyes off me,' she retorted.

'Sorry, I didn't mean to be sharp, it's just that they are only in the other room.' Joel sighed, his voice softening. 'Yes, everything's fine between us. Are you okay?'

'Yes, I'm good. I'm out jogging. Why don't you come and meet me? I'm sure you can make an excuse.' Ava paused slightly and then said softly, 'I just fancied seeing you today.'

Joel was flattered that Ava was chasing him, something that she had never done before and without hesitation, he agreed. His ego had been stroked and he felt a thrill of excitement at the thought of sneaking out to meet his stunning lover.

'Okay, I'll meet you shortly. Let me get ready and I'll text you where we can meet,' he said in as low a voice as he could muster.

Still carrying his coffee, Joel turned, walked past his wife and son, and headed for the stairs. 'I'm off out for a jog. I'm feeling really stiff this morning. I think I need some fresh air and exercise,' he announced.

Cassie hardly even looked up as she muttered 'Okay' and continued her tidying.

As Joel jogged slowly down the back residential streets, criss-crossing his way towards the High Street, his breath appeared strained and uneven. He really should have just said he was going for a walk, although if he had said that Cassie may have suggested joining him. He would just have to get fitter, he thought, as he turned the corner and crossed the main High Street to the Coffee Bean Café on the other side. He could not immediately see Ava as he approached as the windows were steamed up from the contrast with the cooler outside air. He made his way inside and immediately saw her at the back of the room, with her head bent forward, concentrating on her phone, and a yellow patterned mug on the table in front of her. Black coffee, Joel thought and smiled. That was something that they had in common.

Joel ordered his own mug of black coffee, which was offered in a matching red patterned mug, and made his way to the back of the café to join his lover. He slid into the seat to the side of her, his back to the wall and facing the front of the café so that he had a clear view of who was coming in. He smiled broadly at her. 'Hi gorgeous.'

Ava looked up and beamed back at him, leaning forward to blow a silent kiss to him as she did so.

Joel ran, rather than jogged, the last two streets as he made his way home. He and Ava had stayed out far too long, and he knew that it would be difficult for him to justify spending four hours out jogging. His mind whirled as he tried to think up a valid excuse that Cassie would believe. His worried expression relaxed slightly as he thought back to the afternoon. It had been worth it though. The day had been magical and the connection between them had been the strongest he had ever felt, as if they had known each other forever. It was as if they had history together and Joel kept having to remind himself that they had only met a few months ago. Maybe this is what they refer to as love at first sight, he thought. That instant connection that you know in your heart and soul was meant to be. That recognition on some level that this person was placed here to be in your life, to be part of your destiny.

Joel and Ava had finished their coffee and wandered down the High Street to the old antiques centre. Aladdin's Cave was situated in an old warehouse building fronting the river. It was a huge space with several levels, all stuffed with different stallholders and their goods. Not everything was a genuine antique, of course, some of the stalls sold bric-a-brac and vintage clothes, but it was a great place to just wander and lose yourself for a few hours. And that is just what they did, losing themselves in the endless aisles of jewellery, vases, pictures, and anything else you could imagine. There was so much on some stalls that it was almost impossible to take it all in at once. However, they had not really been concentrating on the items, just chatting, and enjoying spending quality time together.

'How do you think Cassie found out?' Ava suddenly asked Joel as they lingered over some coloured glass vases.

Joel was a bit taken aback. Ava was always so abrupt, as if she just couldn't hold in her curiosity, and it just came out whether it was likely to offend or not.

'I have no idea,' Joel shook his head. 'I've been so careful.

Maybe it's a woman's intuition,' and he raised his eyebrows at her in a comical fashion.

'Maybe. There's no obvious reason for her to have found out, other than gut instinct. Maybe she's psychic!' Ava laughed, mimicking his joke, as a deep but very feminine chuckle escaped her lips. Joel couldn't help but smile at the sound. He grinned at Ava but knew it was no laughing matter.

'You might be right. Cassie's not stupid. She's always known things without having been told them. I've often thought it was more than basic instinct, as if she has a heightened awareness of how people are going to behave.'

Joel cast his eyes sideways to look at Ava as he said this, but her stoney face caused him to lose his train of thought. 'What's the matter?' he whispered, thinking that she had seen someone they both knew.

'I don't need to hear how clever your wife is!' Ava snapped at him. 'Everyone has a good instinct, unless you are completely stupid!' and she walked off to make her annoyance known, pretending to look at some little animal figurines in the neighbouring booth.

Joel sighed. How stupid could he have been, praising his wife to his mistress? He followed Ava, slipping his arm around her waist as he caught up with her, and giving her a squeeze. 'Don't be mad with me,' he said, bending down to kiss her on the top of her head, as he drew her to him.

Ava looked up at him and half smiled. 'My fault for being jealous,' she said and pulled him down to her level so that she could kiss him more fully. They locked lips, wrapped in each other's embrace, as the world busied itself around them. Eventually, they pulled apart, Joel looking around to check that they hadn't been seen but relenting to hold Ava's hand this time. Ava smiled at her lover, completely caught in the moment. Maybe I am falling for him, she said to herself, a tinge of excitement causing her to smile a little broader.

For a little while they continued to hold hands but then Joel suddenly got nervous that they would bump into someone they knew, and he gently pulled away with the pretence of looking at a cabinet full of brooches and rings. As his eyes ran along the numerous rows, they fell on an old, tarnished knife about four inches long, tucked away to one side. Instantly, Joel was hooked. Looking closer he could see that it was engraved with tiny squares, each with an individual motif, but the years of neglect had tarnished the metal and a lot of the pattern was obscured with rust. Only small areas could be seen through the grime but the concept of cleaning this historical item and discovering more fascinated Joel, and he was surprised to feel his heartbeat quicken. He wasn't usually emotionally affected in this way by possessions or ornaments, but there was something about this little knife that called to him, and he knew that he had to add it to his military-based collection of items.

After locating the stall holder, an elderly gentleman called Bryan who had incredible knowledge of military memorabilia, and a little negotiation over the price, the carefully bubble-wrapped knife now lay in Joel's jogger pocket. His hand kept searching for it, and he wrapped his fingers around it every now and then as they continued their mooching, He felt a sense of comfort which he couldn't really explain.

Of course, Joel and Ava completely lost track of time and it was not until Ava noticed the large original warehouse clock in the centre of the upper level, that they realised that it was nearly a quarter to three. Joel felt a wave of panic as he realised how long they had been out and how he was going to explain his prolonged absence to Cassie. Ava just smiled at him and told him not to worry. They parted quickly and without much ceremony on the steps of the building as Joel started to run back in the direction of home.

As Ava watched him race off into the distance, her face was blank with a neutral expression, but her stomach was saying something different. She hated the fact that he was going back to Cassie and his son, and she was going home alone. She plugged her earphones back into her ears and headed slowly off in the opposite direction.

As Ava turned her key in the front door lock, the silence of her flat was all-encompassing. As she shut the front door with a thud, putting the chain into place, she stood for a few minutes in the stillness just listening. There was absolute silence. Nobody to greet her with a hug and a kiss, no child or pet running to embrace her, no happy family sounds, just empty palpable silence. Eventually, with a heavy heart, Ava walked down the hall, throwing her keys into a little white pottery bowl she kept on the thin console table that ran almost three-quarters of the length of her hall. Positioned all along the table were silver-framed photos of her family, and she slowed as they caught her eye. Her father in his military uniform, flanked by both of her brothers squinting from the bright sunshine. Her mother kneeling in the garden cutting roses, her head turned to the camera, smiling broadly. A picture of Ava and her brothers splashing in the red paddling pool her father always put out for them on the lawn every summer. Seemingly happy family memories. 'Were we happy?' Ava asked herself aloud, her words shattering the silence and reverberating around her. The contrast of her voice against the silence made the words seem unnecessarily loud. 'Were we really happy?' She repeated the question to herself. She wasn't sure anymore. Only the anxiety and frustration were coming to the fore of her memories, the difficult times when her father was cross with them all, and her flinching when he even spoke to her. It was an involuntary action for the little timid girl, but it infuriated her father, making him shout louder and louder.

Ava had a vivid and frightening memory of the three of them hiding from him behind cardboard boxes and the vacuum cleaner in the cupboard under the stairs, her hands over her ears, trying desperately not to make a sound. They had stayed there for what felt like hours, as her father rampaged around the house, finally slamming the front door as he left for another period away. She remembered her mother coming to open the understairs door and gently helping them out, before wrapping them in blankets and making them all cocoa as a soothing treat. They had cuddled on the sofa all evening, a comforting effort from their mother for normality to return. And normality did return, but those episodes of fear and intimidation had stuck with Ava. Her heart had hardened towards her father and their relationship as she grew older. Before his death, she had hardly spoken to him in years, and when she received the telephone call that he was dying, she had not even bothered to go and see him. She had felt bitter towards him and the hurt he had caused, and just didn't want to see him or talk to him. What would she have said? Why were you so mean and unkind?

Ava shook her head as these old and disturbing memories drifted into her mind. She had been dreaming of her father more and more of late, and it felt uncomfortable. Why was she connecting with him now when they couldn't in life? Was he really protecting her or tormenting her? Ava chuckled to herself but it was cold and humourless. Tormenting her was more like it. Ava's thoughts naturally shifted to her mother as well. She loved her mother – who had always been comforting after the event – but Ava couldn't help but find her weak. Why hadn't she left him and taken them with her? Why hadn't she stood up to him? The questions screeched in her head and she put her hands on her ears again, just like when she was a child, to calm them down. She just couldn't forgive her mother for not protecting them more and allowing her childhood to be so difficult. No wonder she didn't want children of her own. If there was no guarantee that she would be able to give any child an amazing life, then she just wasn't prepared to take that chance. She knew how difficult it could be, and she wasn't prepared to inflict that on anyone. Adults were different, they could look after themselves, but she couldn't bring a child into a troubled situation.

Ava stood in her small square kitchen, wondering what to eat. She always found it difficult to decide what to cook for one. She was an excellent cook and loved giving dinner parties for her friends, but when it came to just her, she really couldn't be bothered. She settled on a poached egg on toast, eating it from a tray on her lap as she watched the latest episode of her current favourite series on Netflix. Once she had finished eating, she showered, dressed in a very elegant pale blue lounge suit, and snuggled under a blanket on her sofa to watch another episode.

Warm and well-fed, she drifted off into a deep sleep. She

could see her father again, gesticulating at her and screwing up his face, but there was no sound. She realised that she couldn't hear anything that he was saying, and that without sound his facial expressions and actions seemed almost comical. Ava started to laugh at him, pointing her finger in a mocking way, and he stopped moving and stood still in her mind's eye. As she continued to wag her finger at him, he began to get smaller. Ava watched fascinated as he seemed to shrink, and eventually, she realised that he was melting into a puddle on the floor. Finally, only his head remained in a pool of what looked like water, but which was highly coloured, with ribbons of different hues running through it. Ava wondered whether it was a pool of energy – his energy – but wasn't sure. Slowly his head seemed to fall through the pool and vanished from sight, and then the pool fell in on itself until nothing was left. Just whiteness and silence. The stillness surrounded her, and she was aware that she too seemed to be falling into the whiteness, but instead of being frightened, she felt cocooned and safe. She was being held and comforted and the longing that it created in her made her want to cry.

Ava woke with a start, tears running down her face, the feeling of comfort and love still holding her firm. As she came awake and realised that she was still wrapped in a warm blanket on her sofa, the intense feeling lingered, and she realised that she was indeed crying. The tears intensified as if there was something she needed to release, and eventually, after a good few minutes of sobbing, she drifted back off to sleep, this time to a much-needed dreamless rest.

Tea Leaves

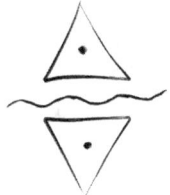

Cassie glanced at the clock, wondering where Joel had got to. She had not really noticed him leaving the house this morning, but the silence was now deafening, and his absence was suddenly very apparent. She got Xander changed and dressed warmly against the cold breeze, placing him in his buggy and putting on her own warm coat, scarf, and gloves against the stormy conditions. She bumped the buggy down the two steps outside her front door and headed off towards her parent-in-law's house. Joel's parents were a great support to Cassie. Patrick was a quiet English man with few words, whilst Sophia was a small, talkative, Portuguese lady whose kindness was not proportional to her stature. They had both always been loving and kind towards Cassie. As soon as Cassie had met them – when she was still at university – she had felt wrapped in warmth and acceptance, and a strong bond had been created between them. She had never known her real father and her mother had been unable to cope for various reasons, so Cassie had been placed into the foster care system from the age of five. The fact that Joel's family had included her with open arms had been amazing and very much appreciated by Cassie. Over the following years, she and Sophia had become firm friends, and Sophia had been a great support after Xander's birth, recognising Cassie's low mood and helping as much as she could. Sophia adored her grandson and, as she was retired, was nearly always available to babysit or run errands for Cassie. Joel's father, Patrick, was also lovely, although a very different character. He would often be quiet just listening to the conversation and observing everyone, but there was genuine warmth there and Cassie was sure that he saw and knew more than he let on. He was also amazing with Xander and there seemed a genuine affection between them on both sides.

Cassie always knew that she would receive a warm welcome from them both and often popped in for coffee or afternoon tea for a chat and that feeling of solidarity and support. Today she felt a need to tell Sophia and Patrick her news, although she would not tell them any of her suspicions about Joel, she wasn't sure how that would be received, and she didn't want to cause any bad feelings. When she arrived at her parent-in-law's house the cobwebs had been well and truly blown away and her cheeks and nose were red from the harsh wind and the exertion. As expected, Cassie and Xander were warmly welcomed and ushered into the large kitchen diner with a lot of hugs and smiles. Xander was scooped up by Patrick, making them both giggle, and placed in a highchair kept there for exactly this reason. Patrick delightedly found some chocolate buttons to keep him happy, and Xander accepted them with relish and a broad smile.

Cassie knew that he was always spoilt by his grandparents and today she wasn't going to argue about the extra sugar.

After half an hour or so Patrick excused himself, giving Xander a firm kiss goodbye on the top of his head. He sensed that Cassie wanted to speak to his wife, and he didn't want to get in the way of that. As he left the room, Sophia began to prepare a fresh pot of tea and chatted about nothing of importance.

A voice called from the hall which led to the back of the house, 'Hello, Sophia. Are you there?'

'I'm here Martha,' Sophia called back. Martha was her next-door neighbour and often popped in for the same reasons as Cassie.

'Hi Cassie, how are you?' asked Martha giving Cassie and then Xander a hug and warm kiss on the cheek as she joined them at the kitchen table. She and Cassie had also become close over the years and Martha was always happy to see her. Martha had been married to Roger for over thirty years and had three daughters of her own, all of them married and living in different parts of the world. Her husband spent most of his time these days in Patrick's shed enjoying the toy soldiers and military campaigns, and Joel had regularly joined the men for a battle or two over the years. The two older men were obsessed with their toys and their wives often despaired. However, Martha's friendship with Sophia had kept her going and was solid and genuine.

'You look well Cassie, what have you been doing?' Martha asked as Sophia busied around, giving her a fresh cup and filling it with the still-warm tea.

'I'm good thanks,' Cassie smiled feeling a lot of affection for this kind lady who had also mothered her over the years and helped fill that void within her. 'I've been quite busy.'

Cassie proceeded to tell her two mother figures all about Sara and the past life regression sessions. They were both fascinated and listened intently to what she had to say. 'Wow! I find that so interesting,' Martha said when Cassie had finished her story. 'I would love a session. You must give me Sara's details; she sounds like a fascinating woman.'

'You know I read the tea leaves, don't you?' she asked Cassie, leaning forward slightly, and peering into her own cup as if to find something interesting there.

'No! I didn't know,' Cassie exclaimed. 'How long have you done that?'

Martha chuckled. 'Oh, Roger thinks it's ridiculous you know, but I've done it since I was about six years old. I learnt from my granny, and she from her granny. We've read the tea leaves in our family for many generations on my mother's side. It's great fun.'

'Martha's often given me a reading,' Sophia added. 'She's very accurate you know.' She nodded at Cassie with a serious expression on her face.

'I had no idea you did that Martha. Will you give me a reading now?'

'Of course. Have you finished your cup? Let's take the filter out of the pot and set our intentions about what we want to receive some information about.' Martha then instructed Sophia to turn the pot three times clockwise and to pour them each a fresh cup allowing some of the tea leaves to flow.

Once they had only a small amount of liquid left in their cups and it was difficult to finish the tea without a mouthful of tea leaves, Martha showed them how to turn the cups upside down using a saucer, and then right side up again ready for a reading.

'Well, I'm definitely flying off to see one of my daughters,' she advised as she scrutinised her own cup carefully. 'There's definitely a plane there,' and she pointed to a section of her cup. 'Emily, I think, as she needs the most help now. I don't think Roger will come with me, so you might have to keep an eye on him, Sophia. Make sure he actually comes out of the shed once in a while!' She chuckled smiling warmly at her friend.

Over the next hour or so Martha read the tea leaves for all three of them, resulting in a great deal of laughter, but also some genuinely accurate messages.

'I can see a completely different life for you in the future, Cassie. You will be much stronger and really empowered. Are you planning on going back to work?' she asked.

'I've thought about it,' Cassie admitted, 'but I really don't feel I could cope with Xander and work now. I'm just not organised enough.'

'You'll get there,' Sophia quipped, patting Cassie's arm and smiling at her daughter-in-law. 'It just takes a bit of time.'

Cassie smiled back knowing Sophia was right. She had felt better somehow since seeing Sara.

'How's Joel?' Martha suddenly asked as she peered into Cassie's cup, turning it repeatedly in her hands.

By the look on Martha's face, Cassie knew she had seen something and was aware that there was tension between them. 'He's okay,' she said as brightly as she could. 'We went to one of his work do's last night,' she added lamely.

'Good,' Martha said with little conviction. 'He's anxious at the moment, torn about something, I think. I sense he feels a little lost. Does that resonate with you?'

Cassie nodded, suddenly not trusting herself to speak.

Sophia looked concerned but didn't say anything. She loved her son dearly, but she knew that he had an angry side to him. Where that came from, she just didn't know. Nothing had happened to him in his childhood that she knew of, and she and Patrick had often said that he just seemed to be born angry. She remembered his rage as a tiny toddler at times – when she had tried to dress him or get him to do something he didn't want to do. It had concerned her then, and it certainly concerned her now. Patrick had been very reassuring, thinking that he would grow out of it with lots of love, but it hadn't quite worked, and she knew that it bothered him as well. However, both their personalities had been a perfect antidote to the anger that Joel seemed to have brought with him into this lifetime, and they had both tried to help Joel tame it over the years, keeping it under control for the most part. Goodness knows what would have happened if he had been born into different circumstances, she thought.

'Hmmm...' Martha said as she pondered Cassie's cup whilst trying to think of something positive to say. Martha had read for hundreds of people over the years. Usually just for fun or as a party trick, but she often knew things or could 'see' situations in her mind's eye. She knew this wasn't comfortable and that there was some tension here. She suspected Joel was seeing someone else from what she could see, and her heart went out to Cassie. She knew Sophia would be heartbroken as well if their marriage fell apart.

'You are going to get some assistance from an unexpected

source,' she advised. 'I think the next few months might be difficult for you, but you will definitely triumph.' She smiled weakly at Cassie, knowing that the path ahead was not going to be easy. As she did so she became aware of a figure in her mind's eye. It was a woman, dressed in a long blue dress, which appeared very lightweight, streaked in red dust around the hem, and a deeper blue patterned scarf wrapped around her head. Martha sensed that she was from a hot climate, and she could see she was red-haired, the copper tresses escaping from around her face, and below the makeshift headdress. She wondered who she was and began to describe her to Cassie.

Cassie's mouth dropped slightly as she took in the description, looking at Sophia for support, before turning back to Martha. From her surprised expression, Martha knew she recognised the woman who had made herself known to her.

'Do you know who it is dear?' Sophia asked, rubbing Cassie's shoulder for support.

'Oh my God!!' exclaimed Cassie. 'It sounds like the woman in my past life regression session. Who is she?' she asked Martha.

Martha looked a little taken aback. 'I'm not sure,' she said softly, 'but let's see if she will give me some more information.' With that, Martha closed her eyes and focused on the figure in her mind's eye. She had been able to see and sense Spirit from an early age, and Spirit people often popped up in her readings. She could sense that the woman was a strong, confident individual with a mind of her own. She could also sense that life was not always easy for this woman, but that she also spoke to Spirit and allowed herself to be protected and guided by this powerful source of energy that surrounds us all.

'She's definitely connected to you in some way, an ancestor maybe. She's here to offer you protection and to guide you now. Guides often come in to help with a particular task or period and she's here for a specific purpose. I feel as if she is trying to tell you something, but I'm not sure what that is,' Martha informed her captive audience of two.

Of course, Martha suspected that the warning was about Joel's affair but didn't want to put that out there and upset these two good friends, so she kept that information to herself. However, the message was so strong that Martha felt she should impart as much of it as possible without revealing the true reason. She wanted Cassie to find this out for herself but also wanted to give her a clue that would help her along the way.

'I want to say that she's some sort of healer. I feel as if she helps people. Maybe like we are doing now, but also with spells and potions. She's not from this country or time though. It feels hot and dusty, and I keep getting an image of red rock faces. She's involved with the dead as well in the sense that maybe she prepares the dead for burial or something. I feel as if she speaks to Spirit though, her psychic energy is really heightened.' Martha paused as she allowed further information to drift into her awareness. Martha knew that if she tried too hard, nothing would come, so she forced herself to relax. She took a deep breath and allowed her shoulders to drop.

Eventually, she said, 'She's trying to warn you.' Cassie gasped slightly.

Martha opened her eyes at the sound. 'Don't panic!' she said reassuringly. 'There's not going to be a disaster. However, she does want you to be more aware of your surroundings and relationships, and to ensure that you stay very present in the now. Focus on the little clues and signs around you. Whatever is going on will change your life but for the better, so don't think the worst. Sometimes events happen, or people come into our lives to change things, to shift us back onto our correct path. At the time they can feel frightening and destructive, but actually it's the Universe trying to move you to the place that you need to be to lead a full and happy life.' She smiled at Cassie and Sophia, completely masking the tendrils of fear that were gently gripping her stomach. She did not want them to see or feel the emotion that was just making itself known. She knew that this woman was scared for Cassie and that she was willing her to be okay, as if she was sending her a warning across time and space. Martha had never received such a strong and clear message before and felt slightly shaken by it, but she certainly wasn't going to allow it to show. She vowed silently to help in any way she could.

'Well, I'm used to a rocky road. Thank you, Martha, that was really interesting.' Cassie's smile was genuine.

'We are both always here for you, Cassie. We can help if you let us,' Sophia added reassuringly. Cassie smiled at the two older women sitting on either side of her, knowing that their concern and offers of help were from the heart, and she felt instantly buoyed.

Cassie was sitting on the sofa cradling a sleeping Xander in her arms as Joel walked through the front door. After a couple of hours at his grandparents and some lunch, Xander was ready for an afternoon nap and was fast asleep. Joel had forced himself to resist rushing into the house hyperventilating and making it obvious he was out of breath, but instead waited a good five minutes just around the corner until he had his breathing under control. He tried to act as nonchalantly as possible as he let himself into the house and called out to Cassie that he was home, tossing his keys into the glass bowl on the table in the hall as he passed. When there was no answer from her, he made his way into the sitting room and seeing her there staring at the television screen, repeated her name as a question. She briefly glanced at him with a furious look on her face and then turned her head back to the wildlife programme that was playing without saying a word. Cassie ignored him completely, not trusting herself to speak, and not wanting to wake Xander at this time either. She suddenly felt exhausted and drained, as if her muscles just would not hold her if she tried to stand up. She knew in her heart that he had been out with someone and her imagination had been running wild. Whilst at Sophia's she had been able to keep the thoughts at bay, but now the emotions that she was feeling were painful and bubbling up to the surface, ready to explode. Cassie struggled to keep them under control and the tears of frustration and pain from flowing.

Joel could see that she was mad and upset and did not know how to respond. He stood there for a few seconds like a rabbit in a headlight, before quickly heading upstairs for a shower. He knew that he had been found out but some defiant streak in him refused to be downtrodden and to feel that he was in the wrong. If she had behaved more like a wife should, then this would not have happened, he reasoned. He knew that he was being ridiculous and unreasonable but his ego just would not let him admit it to himself. There was nothing wrong in him enjoying a few hours with a colleague and he was not going to be made to feel guilty about it.

As he began to undress for his shower, he felt the knife in his pocket – which he had briefly forgotten about – and he placed it on his side table to have a closer look at later. Once Joel was showered and dressed in a clean T-shirt, hoodie and sweatpants, he lay on the bed and contemplated his new purchase. He also felt tired – having had so much exercise that day – but he also knew that he would have to face Cassie again shortly, and the guilt of his actions weighed him down. He picked up the knife thinking that maybe he would stay up in their room for a while and delay the inevitable. He slowly unwrapped his latest purchase and examined it more closely. It was about four inches long and was very tarnished and battered. It appeared to be made of some sort of grey metal, like iron, which was now covered in red rust patches. As Joel used his thumb to rub the side of the pommel, the geometric pattern started to become clearer and he could see that it was made up of repeated squares, each with the same design in the middle. It was a geometric design of two opposite triangles, one upright and one upside down, with a wavy line across the gap in the middle. Joel thought he could also make out circles at the top and bottom, but they were so small, and the knife so dirty, that it was difficult to tell. Joel knew a little about military insignia or coat of arms, but he did not recognise this particular design. However, he did know that the different elements within a motif or insignia reflected important principles or places relevant to the regiment or family that it represented. He examined the details further and reasoned that the wavy line probably represented the sea and indicated a sea-far-ing family or a place on the coast. The triangles probably represented the trinity and a Christian family, he reasoned.

Joel sat up further on the bed as his curiosity was piqued and pulled his laptop in front of him to do some further research whilst he was in self-imposed isolation. What Joel found fascinated him. The triangle was one of the first symbols used to represent the trinity of God, which itself represented all aspects of God as the Father, Son, and Holy Spirit. He also discovered that the circle was also representative of God with no beginning or end, eternal and never-ending, perfection. The diamond, which was formed by the two triangles of the motif, represented ascension, clarity, wisdom and ultimately immortality. Obviously, whoever designed this pattern was clearly religious, believing in God and eternity, Joel mused, and if indeed the wavy line represented a family living or working on the sea, then this was a good representation of a family's morals and their location.

Joel cocked his head slightly listening for any sounds downstairs but he could only hear the slight drone of the television. He wondered what she was doing. Sulking no doubt, he thought harshly, and immediately a wave of guilt swept through him. If she had disappeared all morning and left him on his own, he would be furious. He realised how unfair he was being and, breathing deeply, he tried to think of something that he could do to make amends. Maybe making dinner tonight would help.

He closed his laptop and slid it down the side of the bed. Taking the knife, he made his way down the stairs. He walked to the glass cabinet in the sitting room and placed his new acquisition carefully in line with his other precious items, resolving to clean it later when he had some more time. He wasted some time rearranging the items to accommodate the new knife, before closing the door and turning to face his wife. However, she wasn't there. 'Cassie,' he called. 'Cassie, what do you fancy for dinner tonight?' There was no response and Joel made his way through the house calling her name, before concluding that she had obviously gone out. He checked for Xander's buggy, which was gone, and then in the garage for the car, which was also gone. A knot in his stomach tightened slightly but he pushed any negative thoughts out of his mind and concentrated on a few jobs around the house. Refusing to think too deeply about the situation at hand, Joel sorted out a wash and put it on, cleared up the kitchen and then finished putting up some shelves in the garage which he had meant to do for weeks. As he sorted out a few items and arranged them on the finished shelves an hour or so later, he allowed his thoughts to return to Cassie. He had not heard her come back and he was beginning to worry. Had she left him? As this thought flashed across his mind, his stomach tightened even further and he wiped his sweating palms on his sweatpants.

Finally, with a heavy heart, he picked up his phone and scrolled to his messages. There were none. He stared at the screen for a while before dialling her number and placing the phone to his ear. As he listened to the insistent ringing, the knot twisted and tightened.

'Hello,' Cassie's voice sounded flat, and he realised that he was shocked that she'd answered.

'Where are you?' he questioned. 'I was going to make us something for dinner, or we could get a takeaway. What do you prefer?'

There was a pause on the other end of the line before

Cassie quietly said, 'Whatever you think. I'll be back in about forty minutes.'

Joel realised he'd been holding his breath and he let it out slowly. 'Great, I'll see you then.'

Thank goodness she was coming home. The relief highlighted how stupid he'd been, and he realised how much he really did love his wife and son. Sleeping with a work colleague was a stupid thing to do and, as the waves of guilt kept crashing over him, he vowed to finish it with Ava. He set about preparing a cottage pie ready for Cassie's return.

Forty minutes later, almost to the dot, Joel could hear Cassie sliding her key into the lock. He rushed into the hallway to greet her, being overly helpful as they manoeuvred the buggy, gently lifting his sleeping son out and carefully taking off his all-in-one sleepsuit. Xander hardly stirred and Joel motioned to Cassie without speaking that he would put him straight down in his cot to continue sleeping.

When he got back to the kitchen Cassie was sitting at the table nursing a glass of red wine. Joel hurried about, placing the piping hot pie on a mat on the table, setting out plates and cutlery, and finally serving her a portion. Cassie said nothing, just watching him as he fell over himself to be an exemplary husband. It was so obvious that he felt guilty, but exactly what about, she thought. What had he been up to, and who with? Her thoughts kept returning to the red-haired woman at the work event for some reason. She wasn't sure why, she really didn't have any concrete reason, but something was telling her that she was the other woman. Cassie felt deflated and emotional, struggling to eat the meal put in front of her, not even really tasting it.

Life Goes On

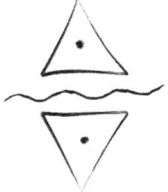

The next few weeks were busy and full of preparations for Christmas. Sophia had invited Cassie, Joel, and Xander for Christmas Day, hoping to take some pressure off them and wanting a happy family atmosphere for everyone to enjoy. Martha and Roger had also been invited. They usually went to one of their daughters, but Martha had only just returned from seeing Emily in Utah so they did not feel they could justify another trip so quickly. Instead, they had gratefully accepted Sophia's invitation to join them for Christmas lunch. Joel's father had also, of course, been there, as had his Aunt Selene and her husband, also called Patrick but whom they all called Pat to avoid confusion. It was an older crowd but having Xander had helped to balance the energy. Cassie had really enjoyed herself and had the opportunity to relax, whilst Xander was kept busy with Sophia and her doting guests. She and Joel felt surprisingly comfortable and happy and there had been a lot of laughter and genuine enjoyment. Sophia was pleased to see them looking so together, but Martha was not so easily convinced. She kept her thoughts to herself, of course. This was her friend's house, and she didn't want to see her upset in any way, but she could sense something else between Cassie and Joel. She wasn't entirely sure what it was, but there was a different energy underlying their happy personas. The red-haired woman had also made her presence known a couple of times during the day, much to Martha's surprise. When Martha gave readings, she would open herself up to the messages and guidance from Spirit, but when it was her own time, she had learnt to firmly close the door to them, overwise she would get no peace at all. However, this woman was strong and very persistent.

'I know, I know,' Martha had silently told her at one point during the day. 'I've told her that she needs to be careful and watch her back. I don't want to scare her either.'

There was a pause. 'Why does she need to be scared?' Martha had tentatively asked following this exchange. The resulting answer in flashes of images, clearer than she had ever seen before, had scared and unsettled Martha. She was clearly being shown past life events, but they seemed violent and fatal.

'Who are you to Cassie by the way?' she had asked the woman. 'Oh! I've never felt that before! How interesting.'

'Martha, are you with us?' Sophia asked her friend. 'You seem miles away?'

'Oh sorry. Just daydreaming a little.' Martha smiled and accepted the mince pie and cream being handed to her. However, her mind instantly went back to the information she had just been given. She had never known a person contact themselves from a past life with a warning for their current life. She felt slightly confused as to whether that was even possible, maybe she'd got it wrong? I wonder if I could have a conversation with Sara, she thought to herself.

As soon as Sara met Martha, she knew that she was a powerful spiritual presence and that the image that she gave off was not what was hidden underneath. Martha had an amazing energy and Sara had no doubt that she would have a very powerful and revealing session. They had talked beforehand of Martha's experience with Spirit – which she'd had since she was a child – and her curiosity around past lives – although she had never really explored that area. Martha had told Sara all about her experiences with the red-haired woman and queried whether it was possible to warn yourself through time and space. Sara had to admit that she had never come across such a situation, but she couldn't see why it wasn't possible. Sara was also very careful not to tell Martha any information from her sessions with Cassie, but immediately could see that they would benefit from talking and vowed to suggest a meeting to Cassie the next time they met.

'I suppose every time that you have a past life session you are obtaining information from that lifetime, and if things weren't successful then you are able to see how you need to change things in your current life. As to whether you can give yourself a warning, I don't see why not. You are connecting to the energy of that lifetime, and energetically that could be a warning to change your perspective or change your ways. Yes, I think it's possible,' Sara finally concluded.

'I've never had a past life session,' Martha advised. 'It's always fascinated me, but I've never gone back to see who I was.'

'Well today's the day,' Sara smiled broadly at her and clapped her hands. 'I'm really excited to start.'

As Sara expected, Martha went quickly and easily into a deep trance, and Sara expertly guided her through an induction and into a past life which would help Martha understand the present events.

Martha's breathing was slow and gentle, and Sara watched it intently as she waited for her to describe her surroundings. Time ticked by and after a couple of prompts, Martha had still not spoken. Sara had experienced this before, and it was either caused by the information flooding in and the client just not relaying it, or the client had gone so deeply into a trance that she couldn't speak.

Sara began to bring Martha up from the deep trance that she believed she was in, when Martha suddenly said, 'Sorry I was getting so much information I just let it flow.'

'That's okay,' Sara said. 'Do you want to tell me about it?'

'I'm a nanny,' she said, 'for a wealthy family. It looks Italian somehow, or somewhere like that. The sun is shining, and the house is all white walls and tiled floors. I get a real sense that it's by the sea, you can almost smell it in the air.' There was a pause and then Martha said, 'They also have a coat of arms or something similar which shows the sea, I think. It's two triangles with a wavy line between them. It's on the tiles and in the walls at the front of the property. It's very important to them to have that and be seen to have that by the community. I feel like there is a lot of pride with this family.'

Martha paused before saying, 'I think most of them died.'

'Do you know how?' Sara prompted.

'Well, I think the parents were killed in some sort of carriage or covered cart that they were travelling in. It overturned and they were both crushed. How awful,' she concluded.

'The children were left with me and other staff in the house. They were in their late teens and the boy took charge. He was very young, but I also think he was married as well. There's another woman who I get the feeling was a bit up herself, if you pardon the expression!'

Sara smiled at the description, 'I know what you mean.' she reassured.

'Yes, his wife. She's also very young and very jealous of the daughter of the household. There is a lot of rivalry between them.' Martha paused again for a while before saying, 'She's only after the family money.'

As Martha continued to describe the house that she lived in with this family, and the family that lived there, Sara could immediately see the similarities to Cassie's descriptions of her Roman life, although she had not mentioned the sister-in-law yet. She wondered whether there was a connection.

'Tell me about the children that you look after.'

There was a pause and then Martha said, 'I think one of them died not long after the parents.'

Sara didn't reply but waited as Martha gained more insight.

'Yes, the girl died, and this is awful, but I think she was murdered with a knife to the stomach,' Martha gasped slightly as if about to sob and her right hand came up to her stomach as if to protect herself. 'How sad,' she muttered and then went silent again.

Sara patiently waited for Martha to speak again. 'She was

murdered by her brother,' Martha suddenly exclaimed. 'Stabbed in the stomach.'

'Can you sense the energy of that girl?' Sara asked. 'Do you know her in this lifetime?'

There was a pause and then Martha said, cocking her head slightly to one side as if processing some information, 'I think it's Cassie.'

'Really!' Sara pretended to be surprised. 'That's so interesting that you were together then, and you are now.'

'Yes, but she was murdered. That's awful and how does that relate to now?'

There was a pause, and Sara held her breath slightly as she knew Martha would be tapping into the brother's energy.

Martha's hands went to her face in surprise, 'It's Joel!'

After the session, Sara and Martha sat drinking tea, allowing Martha to come back into the present. They discussed the information that had come to light.

'Of course, it doesn't mean that Joel will try and kill Cassie in this lifetime,' Sara explained to Martha, 'just that they may have this history which needs to be resolved. They will both have intense emotions from that time and although they may play out again, I suspect it will be in a different but parallel way.'

'Yes, I'm sure you're right, thank goodness. I wonder where I fit in though. I obviously loved them both and cared for them in that lifetime, administered to their every need, through sickness and health. I could see myself putting a poultice on the wound when Cassie was hurt, so I'm assuming I was a nurse of some sort as well.'

'That's interesting. Maybe you're here again to support

Cassie emotionally and spiritually this time, rather than physically?' Sara suggested. 'There will be lots of parallels, I'm sure.'

'Yes, that's resonating with me. I've known Cassie for some years now and I'm always there for her as support, so that makes sense.' Martha paused as she thought through the connections. 'I love Joel as well, of course. I've known him since he was a baby. And I love Sophia and Patrick as well. I wouldn't want anything to happen to any of them.'

'No, of course not.' Sara patted her arm.

It was now early February, with Christmas being well and truly over and the dreary month of January having passed with little incident. Cassie sat with her legs tucked under her on Sara's comfy couch, Xander asleep in his buggy by her side. Cassie had not managed to get many sessions in over the Christmas period, and she was anxious to get back to the life that now echoed frequently through her dreams. She knew that if she could unravel it, then it would disappear, and her sleep would settle.

'I'm sorry I had to bring him. Sophia has gone shopping with Martha, and I didn't want to cancel after such a long break,' she explained to Sara.

'No problem. Hopefully, he will sleep through it all,' Sara reassured her friend, although she was a little concerned. If Xander woke at a crucial moment it might adversely affect the session, but she put her concerns to one side. Her friend had experienced going into trance and knew what to expect, so that helped. Cassie was also having trouble sleeping, with vivid dreams repeatedly taking her back to the past lives she had seen, so there was something that they needed to clear.

Cassie settled down on Sara's cushions, feeling really relaxed even with Xander in the room. She glanced over at her sleeping son, smiled slightly, and closed her eyes in preparation. She could smell the lovely essential oils that Sara had put in the diffuser in readiness for the session, and the familiar scent took her deeper into a relaxed state. There was now a connection between the two, the scent and accompanying relaxation, which helped considerably.

Sara slowly and calmly guided her with skill back into a deep trance and Cassie found herself in a busy market scene, one she hadn't seen before. There were a lot of people milling around, but a flash of red hair caught her attention, and as she followed the image, she was sure that this was the red-haired woman she had seen before. There was a real familiarity to her and Cassie, to her surprise, felt a loving bond to this strange character from another time and space. Cassie followed the woman as she strolled between the different stalls, smiling at the traders, and carefully selecting various items which she placed in a woven bag attached to her waist. This time she had no shawl over her head and the bright sun made her copper tresses shine in such a way that, at times, it was blinding. Again, the distinct hue of her hair and the tricks of light seemed to exaggerate the colour, and Cassie felt that it was clearly trying to tell her something. It again seemed to be the only colour in an otherwise neutral scene and the reason for this bugged Cassie. As she explained this to Sara later, she likened it to a symbol, or perhaps a warning. As soon as she said the word Cassie felt such a strong response that she knew that it was correct. This woman was trying to get her attention by sending her a warning across time and space, across many lifetimes. Why? What was the warning about and what did she need to know?

Cassie continued to watch the woman as she made her way from the market, a large open-air space in the fierce midday sunlight, into narrower darker passageways which appeared to be formed between walls of rock. There were no bricks or stones making up these walls, but what appeared to be actual rock faces. They were smooth and red in colour and Cassie guessed that she was in a hot desert area, but she wasn't sure where. Egypt came immediately to mind, but she knew it wasn't quite right. As she continued to watch, the woman weaved her way through the darkened passageways out of the sun, following a series of upward zig zags. It was clear that the woman was very familiar with this place, this city built into the rock, as her pace was quick and purposeful. Finally, she came to a stop and pulled a pale blue scarf out of her bag, which she carefully wrapped around her nose and mouth, her large dark eyes peering out from the folds of cloth.

Cassie struggled at first to see where she was or why she had come to this place. It took time but eventually, the imagery cleared enough for Cassie to see that the woman appeared to be standing in front of a shallow cave, wider than a ledge and hewn again from the rock itself. There were different bands of colour this time, as if several layers of sediment had occurred in quick succession, with shades of cream, orange, and the usual red. There was also a crystalline band of white which appeared to glisten slightly.

The woman pulled a small shallow bowl from her robes and placed what looked like small yellow stones into it. Cassie realised that it must be the frankincense resin that she had used before in her rituals. The woman proceeded to light them, and then several beeswax candles which she wedged into various spaces along the edge of the ridge. The smoke from the resin drifted lazily across the scene as the woman knelt in front of the cave, seemingly in prayer. With some gentle questioning from Sara, Cassie was able to look more fully at the scene and could see the red rock and dust that now coloured the woman's knees and the hem of her skirt. The natural light appeared to be fading and Cassie got the impression of dusk, as the shadows lengthened, and the candlelight caused the now familiar flickering of light and shadows to play across the scene. The woman was chanting and moving her hands as if tracing symbols in the air. Eventually, Cassie was able to make out a shape lying on the floor of the shallow cave and realised, with a start, that it looked like several naked bodies laid out side by side on a piece of cloth. The shapes began to morph as Sara took Cassie a little deeper into trance, allowing her to relax to a completely different level and to obtain more information from the scene unfolding in front of her, and from her guides. The bodies would be left open to the elements, allowing the vultures and birds of prey to pick at their flesh until only bones were left. Although it felt incredibly macabre to Cassie, she knew that this was part of the woman's tradition and the beginning of the journey for the souls of the departed into the afterlife. Asking her guides, Cassie was able to understand how the bodies had been anointed and bathed with oils. It was almost as if she had a visual flash of the process taking place and was acutely aware of the essences being used and a heady mixture of scents hanging in the air. She knew that one was myrrh, the word just popped into her head, and another was the word 'elemi' which joined the first, and she played with them as she mused over their joint meaning. As she mentally asked herself why this information was coming to her, she instantly received an answer. These were the names of oils that were used while preparing the body. Elemi was used to strengthen the connection of the deceased with their ancestral lineage, so that the soul easily travelled over to the other side. As she digested this, a sweet, honey and lemon-tinged aroma began to encircle her. She was surprised and wasn't sure whether this was from the diffuser in the room, or whether she was able to smell the scent that wafted across time and space. She sniffed several times, taking in this warm spicy scent and allowing the connection to draw her further in. As she did so, she was aware that the relationship between the living and the dead was extremely important to these people and that the dead remained a constant presence in their lives. The woman had been visiting for the relative of a loved one who had passed, using oils and incense in reverence to their long line of ancestors that connected them from this lifetime to the next, and ensuring that no soul was stuck or needed assistance to commence their journey. As these thoughts formed and then gently dissipated, Cassie slowly became aware of a line of figures stretching away across space and time. All different faces, figures, and characters. Just as the image began to fade, Cassie almost felt as if she could see herself at the end of the line, peering curiously around the shoulder of the figure in front of her. She smiled at the comical nature of this, shaking her head slightly at how absurd this seemed. A further thought came into her head, which startled her slightly, and she put it aside for later. However, her heart began to race with the realisation.

Cassie was able to explain to Sara that this was a burial site and that the whole of the city in which this woman lived was an interplay of the living and the dead. The concept of people living near their dead was alien to Cassie, and leaving a dead body exposed to the elements and predators on a rock ledge seemed even stranger to her, but she knew that the connection was incredibly important. She also knew that this woman was experienced with such work, and that to her it was the highest honour to prepare those who had passed and to send their souls across the veil. As the light faded into night, the scene slowly disappeared, and Sara brought the session to an end.

'What did you make of that?' Cassie asked Sara as she pulled herself into a seated position and accepted a glass of water.

'It was very interesting and so powerful,' Sara stated. 'I know a little of ancient cultures and the Nabateans were such a people who had a relationship with their dead. Your woman sounds like a priestess who would help souls transition. Mary Magdalene was also one – I can't remember what they are called. I'll look it up though and let you know.'

'I think I'll speak to Alice about it,' Cassie said.

Sara nodded in agreement. 'Of course. She'll know or she'll be able to point you in the right direction.'

'I texted her a while back before Christmas to go for a drink, but we just couldn't find a convenient time. I'll try her again. Do you want to come as well?' Cassie asked Sara.

'Yes, I'd love to. I haven't seen Alice for a while, and I'd love to hear what she has to say,' Sara stated.

'Okay, let's organise a date.' The two women smiled at each other.

Xander was still fast asleep as Cassie gathered her things together. As she did so, her gaze fell on the little bottles of essential oil in Sara's room.

'You didn't have your diffuser on today?' she asked questioningly.

'No, I completely forgot to be honest,' Sara confirmed.

Cassie looked at her in surprise, her mouth slightly open. 'I'm sure I could smell the oils as we started the session!'

'No, I didn't have it on,' Sara said, looking at her friend. 'You can see it's not plugged in,' and she lifted the plug to show Cassie.

'I was sure it was your diffuser. It helped me to relax and connect to the session.'

Sara shook her head, smiling, and raised her shoulders and palms upwards, in a gesture of confusion. 'I might put it on now in any event. I've got some elemi and you can see whether you like it.' She busied herself, preparing the diffuser, plugging it in and dropping a couple of drops of oil into the water.

As the distinct aroma of the oil wafted over Cassie, she felt such a recognition that it shook her. She stood looking at her friend as she took in deep breaths of the aroma. 'Are you okay?' asked Sara, a quizzical look coming over her face as her friend seemed almost in a trance again.

Cassie didn't answer immediately but kept taking in the familiar aroma, seemingly transported straight back to that strange city. 'I know this is silly,' she started, 'but this is the scent

I could smell in the session. I don't know how I know that, but just smelling it again brings such a recognition. I thought you'd put your diffuser on in the middle of the session the smell was so strong to me.' She paused slightly, 'I'm sure that there was something else though as well, something woodier.'

'I think it's called clairessence,' Sara said. 'When you are given smells from Spirit. The name of the other oil will come to you, I'm sure. Once you have a session, further information often comes to you in the following days, maybe in your dreams.'

It was only later after Cassie and Joel had enjoyed an Italian-inspired tea and had put Xander to bed together, that Cassie had a moment to herself. Joel was going out for a few drinks at their local pub with an old school friend, one of the few that he had retained over the years. Cassie, having declined the offer to join him, curled up on the sofa to complete this session's entry in her unicorn journal. The thought that he might be meeting a woman had come to her instantly as he had revealed his plans, but as he had also invited her along, she concluded that he was probably telling the truth this time. He had been very attentive the last few weeks since Christmas, and Cassie was grateful for the change in him, although a little wary.

The baby monitor crackled slightly as Cassie sipped her welcomed cup of mint tea. She had turned off all the lights except for the side lamp, giving the room a subdued and gentle glow. She wanted some peace and relaxation and sighed deeply in the stillness as she settled down to write her experiences and thoughts.

As she wrote out the relationship that the Nabateans had with their dead, recounting the words which had just seemed to appear in her head, she remembered the symbol. It had come to her during the session but she had put it to one side to muse over later. The symbol swam before her eyes again: two triangles opposite each other, with a wavy line in between. Heaven and Earth she mumbled. It represents the connection between Heaven and Earth, the dead and the living and how they are only separated by a thin divide. How interesting, she thought. But how did that connect to her first session, which was a totally different time and country as far as she could make out?

She flicked back through the entries she had made, the first session where she was being hunted by her brother and the tile motif, the second where she had first met the red-haired woman making some sort of figures and with symbols on her face, and now the same woman visiting and praying over the dead. This woman was obviously someone of knowledge about the departed and how to send them safely on their way, but also of rituals and other acts that Cassie was sure had not been fully explained to her yet. She felt such a fondness for this woman, a bond almost, and somehow her thoughts and wisdom seemed to be seeping into her psyche. Random thoughts such as the rituals of the Nabateans just kept coming into her head, as if they shared some common flow of information. The thought had come to her in the session that they might be connected, and now she voiced it.

'Maybe she's an ancestor of mine.' Cassie smiled at the thought, her eyes lighting up in a way that she had never experienced in this lifetime.

Cassie quickly went to check on Xander but found him sleeping soundly on his back, his arms and legs spreadeagled across his cot mattress. His cosy sleepsuit keeping him warm and snug.

As she came back to her seat on the sofa, and her relaxing tea, she reached for a book on essential oils which she had ordered from Amazon after visiting Sara last time. She hadn't had a moment to read it, but her interest was now heightened, and she wanted to understand more about these ancient oils. She became captivated as she began to read, learning about how the oils were made, and their various uses. She found the entry on elemi and was fascinated to find that it was used to help transition the dead. 'How on earth did I know that?' she said aloud to herself.

Cassie was not a gullible person. She was aware that sometimes information from a film or book could stick somewhere in the memory banks until it was triggered into being again. But this time she genuinely did not remember any information coming her way about essential oils. She knew she would have remembered that, and she didn't know the name elemi. This felt like a memory, but not of this lifetime, and that both startled and excited Cassie. She was fascinated about how her experiences with Sara were unfurling and she was excited to find out more.

As she read on, one name seemed to jump out at her and she just couldn't seem to get it out of her mind. She read the entry:

Spikenard was an ancient oil, leading us across the veil to be with those already departed. Its use can help us to receive messages from spirit and to unravel the mysteries of the soul.

Cassie was fascinated by these words and knew instinctively that this was the deeper, woodier, notes that she had smelled. She spent the next two hours devouring as much information as she could.

Eventually, having checked on Xander again, she sank back into the sofa and asked to be connected again to the woman. If

Martha was able to connect to her in her mother-in-law's kitchen, maybe she could connect to her now? I can't keep calling her 'the woman', Cassie thought as she drifted down into a deep state of relaxation.

Since becoming a mother, Cassie always had one ear open for the slightest sound that her child might utter, and would be instantly alert should Xander need her, but she was also able to relax to a very deep state following her regular sessions with Sara. The work that she had done had seemed to trigger a remembrance in her of all things spiritual, and she was able to not only relax into a trance-like state easily and effortlessly, but to know things as well. Thoughts and images seemed to be popping into her awareness of late, surprising her at times, but becoming more and more vivid. Cassie found it exciting, and it was this that propelled her forward, gently moving the fear out of her way and allowing her to relish in anything metaphysical. Her progress was rapid as this newly-remembered information began to flow to her.

She found herself back with the woman sitting cross-legged on the floor of what Cassie presumed was her home. It was simple and sparse, seemingly hewn out of the red rock so that there was a tinge of red to the light. She was aware of the odd item of wooden furniture and personal items dotted about. The feel was of a functional safe place to be. There was no luxury, but Cassie knew it was where this woman felt the safest.

The woman's red hair flowed loosely over her shoulders, glowing a deep red and mesmerising Cassie with its rich hue. There was such a depth to the colour that Cassie felt it had a consciousness of its own, a story only it could tell. As she raised her head so she could see the woman's face, she saw that she had again drawn symbols on her skin, one between her eyes and one on each cheek. As she watched, the symbols seemed to shift and vibrate as three-dimensional versions, and what had initially appeared black, now showed a myriad of colours shimmering and glistening. It was as if the symbols also had a life of their own, a mesmerising depth and presence as they vibrated on their own frequency.

The woman was chanting again, rhythmically swaying from her hips over one of her effigies. Cassie watched her, holding her breath at the clarity of the vision, which was morphing into life before her 'eyes'. As she did so, she began to hear the chant that the woman was making. The sound created a deep resonance which vibrated through her, and she seemed to know just what the woman was thinking. She was making a curse doll, creating a tiny effigy of someone who needed to be bound. Manifesting negative energy towards that person, but only to the extent that they back away and leave the space clear. It was about love and boundaries, Cassie thought. Love rivals playing games and trying to control each other's lives. Cassie also realised that the effigy was made of wax, not clay, so that it could be burnt, leaving no trace of its existence. As the woman's movements accelerated, Cassie moved forward, gently picking up the effigy in her hand. Her movements were slow, almost unbelieving that she could do so, but experimenting with what was possible. She gingerly held the doll in her fingers, feeling the waxy texture and turning it instinctively three times in her palm. She noted that she seemed to do this with purpose but wasn't sure of the reason.

Eventually, she let it go, placing it carefully on the ground in the scene in front of her. She realised that she was still holding her breath, not wanting this incredibly vivid three-dimensional experience to disappear, and she finally let out a full breath. Her breathing quickened as she tried to catch it again and gain some control. Eventually, the woman stopped chanting and picked up the bowl of frankincense resin, wafting the smoke over the effigy with one of her hands. She then placed the little figure on a piece of rough-looking cloth and added a few sprigs of a herb to the mix. She wrapped the effigy carefully, tying the little package up with a piece of twine, and placed it neatly on a ledge. As she did so, Cassie could see that there was a whole row of similar little packages, and she knew that these were all ready for collection by the woman's clients. An array of curse dolls and little tablets with written spells, mixed with a heady scent of spices and herbs, representing assistance for people needing help in some way. This woman was a witch, Cassie thought, but instantly knew that wasn't the right word. There was more to this woman, a compassion and love for her people. There was goodness in her heart, and she knew how to manipulate energy, how to play with it for her desired outcome. There was an element of magic, Cassie thought, tilting her head and smiling slightly. She loved that thought and she knew it was right somehow. There was also a very strong connection to Spirit, a constant source of information that this woman was able to tap into. Maybe we have lost those talents over time, but we all have those abilities if only we woke up to ourselves, Cassie thought. She mulled over her train of thought for a little while, hoping that the right term for the woman would pop into her head, but nothing came. Cassie took a final look at the woman, taking in as much detail as she could before the imagery faded. As it did so, the woman quickly handed her a little package like the ones on the shelf, before totally disappearing.

Cassie looked down at the little package sitting in the palm of her hand, folded her hand over it and then drifted off. Eventually, she found herself coming back into her own time and felt her familiar sofa beneath her. She slowly opened her eyes, feeling very spacey, not sure how long she had been sitting there. She stared at the ceiling, not really seeing it, but rerunning the information in her head that she had just been given. As the baby monitor sprang into action she instantly sat up and made her way to Xander's room, as if on autopilot. Xander was still sleeping soundly, muttering to himself in his sleep, and as Cassie went to pull his door a little further shut, she realised that she was holding something in her hand. As she looked down, opening her hand to reveal what was sitting there, a gasp of surprise and shock left her lips.

The Apport

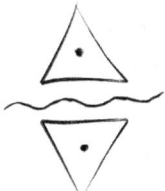

'Oh, my goodness. How exciting. It's an apport! I've heard about them but never experienced it. Tell me exactly what happened.'

Cassie laughed at her friend's excitement and explained again the events of the night before, and how the little package that now sat in front of them on the coffee table had appeared out of nowhere. She explained how the woman had handed it to her in her mind's eye, and suddenly it had just appeared in her physical hand.

Cassie still couldn't believe that it had happened and kept running the events through her mind as if she had missed something and was fooling herself in some way. But the little package had just appeared, seemingly out of thin air. The two friends sat in silence for a while just staring at the package, as if something else was going to happen.

'Have you opened it?' Sara asked.

'Not yet. I thought I'd wait to open it with you.'

'Thank you,' Sara said with genuine gratitude. 'This is so exciting!'

Cassie smiled at her friend. 'Do you want to open it?'

Sara looked a little startled. Cassie could almost see her thinking through the options, as to whether she should or shouldn't open the package.

'I'm not sure if that would be a good idea. The woman wanted you to have it, didn't she.'

'The Magus!' Cassie suddenly said.

'What?' asked Sara. 'The what?'

'The Magus. That's what we need to call her. Not the woman or a witch. She's a Magus,' Cassie concluded.

'Okay, the Magus. I like that. Let's open it.' Sara paused for a moment. 'Shouldn't we document it? Maybe I should video you opening it, so we have some evidence. Alice would kill us if we didn't,' she added.

'Why will we need evidence? We can't show anyone this, can we? They won't believe me, and they will think I've gone completely mad.' Cassie looked slightly alarmed. 'This is just between you and me, Sara. For now, at least. I might tell Sophia and Martha but other than that let's keep it to ourselves.' Cassie looked intently at her friend willing her to agree.

'Well, I do think you should tell Alice. She would be fascinated. After all, if this is a genuine apport, and I'm sure it is, then it will date from another time and Alice could get all sorts of information from the cloth and the twine.' Sara looked at Cassie with a concerned look on her face. 'I do think you should tell Alice,' she concluded, turning back to study the package again.

'Okay, fair enough. We'll video it for Alice and then let her have the different parts to research. You're right, she will be fascinated.'

'Great!' exclaimed Sara. 'Okay, I'm ready,' and she held her mobile phone up to record the grand opening.

Cassie nodded at her friend as she slowly leant forward so that she could open the package while Sara continued filming. For some reason, she suddenly seemed nervous to touch it more than she had to. Cassie gently pulled the string knot undone and allowed the rough square of hessian to gently unfold by itself. Inside were a few sprigs of herbs and the strange little wax figure of a woman, kneeling and with her wrists and ankles tied, which Cassie had seen before.

'I don't know why I'm nervous,' Cassie said. 'I saw her make up the package, so I know exactly what's in it.'

Sara was now kneeling on the floor in front of the coffee table, her nose a few inches from the wax effigy sitting on its square mat of material. 'Wow! I can't believe it. It's amazing and a bit creepy all at the same time.' She moved her head away from the figure, 'And it's a bit mind-blowing, to be honest,' she added. 'She's given you a binding spell to make that woman lose interest in Joel. I never thought I'd see an apport so close. A gift from Spirit, and in this case from the Magus. Physical matter just appearing out of nowhere.'

Sara carefully viewed the little figure from all sides as she continued to film, moving it around with a pencil so as not to touch it and change any of its energy and properties. Eventually, she said, 'So are you going to burn it?'

'Yes, I suppose so,' said Cassie. 'We'll have to find the right time and place.'

The two looked at each other and nodded, and then both stared back at the effigy in silence.

A couple of days later they found themselves tucked into a small booth at the back of their favourite wine bar with Alice. They had finally found a convenient time for them all to catch up, and they were determined to use the time to pick Alice's brains.

'Magus,' Alice said. 'Yes, I've heard that term but it's masculine. I think the feminine should be Maga. It means a witch, a magician, a priestess.'

Cassie smiled, 'That sounds about right. It was the masculine term I was given though.'

'That's interesting. Maybe she was viewed as an equal to men. A Magus would officiate over life ceremonies, like birth, marriage and death, as well as helping people with their problems,' Alice explained. 'It all sounds interesting. And you see the Magus, do you?' Alice asked, raising her right eyebrow slightly.

Cassie laughed, 'Don't say it like that! I've not gone completely mad yet, honestly!' All three of the women laughed out loud.

'Absolutely not!' said Sara. 'You're tapping into a past life and being given information from the Magus that you obviously need at this time. I find it thrilling.'

'I do too,' Alice added, 'although I don't understand it really. Sara has been telling me all about these things for years, but I never seem to quite get my head around it all. Too much of a scientist I think,' and she shrugged her shoulders. 'However, I absolutely respect your years of experience,' she said smiling at her friend, 'Sara, you're the expert in all this stuff.'

'Well, there's something else we wanted to talk to you about,' Sara said, and as she did, Cassie placed the little package on the table in front of them, carefully ensuring that the table wasn't wet in any way before doing so.

'What's that?' Alice asked as she moved her head closer to the item to view it more clearly.

'It's an apport!' Sara exclaimed. 'The Magus gave it to Cassie the other night.'

'What do you mean, she gave it to Cassie. I thought the Magus was someone that you see in your mind's eye?' Alice looked at Cassie with a quizzical expression.

'It is,' Cassie nodded, and then smiling, she said, 'but last night she handed this to me across time and space. I saw it in my meditation. I saw her hand it to me and then when I came to, in my own sitting room, it was in my hand.'

There was a long silence as Alice looked at them both in surprise, at the package, and then back to the girls.

'You're kidding me!' she said but there was no conviction in her voice. Cassie and Sara slowly shook their heads at her in unison. 'Oh, my goodness! I've heard of these things but never experienced it. Wow! A present from a different time.' She paused. 'Maybe I should get this dated by a colleague of mine. It would be fascinating to just get that affirmation.'

Cassie nodded. 'Yes, we thought you would want to do that. It will be really interesting to see what she can find out. How long would that take though?'

'Well, I can go and see her this week. She's only down the corridor at work from me. Why?'

'Well, I want to put it to use. After all, the Magus gave it to me to get rid of Joel's girlfriend, so I'm going to use it for exactly that.'

Alice started, putting her hand outstretched in front of her. 'Stop!' she said, a little dramatically. 'Firstly, I only need a small part of the corner of the material for the dating, and secondly, what girlfriend?'

Over a few glasses of wine, Cassie proceeded to explain to Alice what had been going on in her life. The post-natal depression that she had been experiencing, the affair that Joel was obviously having, and the fascinating sessions she had been attending with Sara. It was difficult to explain in places and felt a bit fanciful at times, but with Sara reassuring her and adding to the story as they went, she was able to give a good account.

'Gosh, I'm sorry you went through all that without me knowing, Cassie. You should have called me, I'm always here if you need a chat,' she patted Cassie's hand. 'I wonder why the Magus is helping you though?' Alice asked.

'I'm not sure,' Cassie said, 'but I wonder if she's an ancestor of mine or something.'

'Well, she's definitely trying to warn you,' Sara added.

'What does red hair remind you of?' Alice suddenly asked Cassie, leaning forward slightly to peer into her face as she spoke.

Cassie looked at Alice, her stomach suddenly tightening. 'I'm not sure,' she said slowly. She was aware of something flickering in her subconscious but the wine was blurring her clarity.

'I think the Magus is trying to reference red hair, or someone you know with red hair.' Alice concluded. 'I think you need to find that connection. That's your next clue.'

'Yes, good idea. And then you need to use the effigy. Do you want us to help you?' Sara asked, obviously wanting to be involved. Cassie chuckled. 'Of course. I wouldn't know what to do otherwise,' and Sara grinned, squeezing Cassie's arm in excitement.

'Can I help as well?' Alice asked tentatively.

'Of course!' Sara and Cassie chimed in unison and the three friends dissolved into a fit of giggles, instantly easing the tension.

After another hour or so of planning how they could prepare to use the effigy, letting Alice watch the video Sara had taken when the package was initially opened, and after snipping a small corner of the material off for Alice to take to work, the three friends departed for their own homes. 'It's been so lovely to see you both,' Alice added as they had a group hug. 'We haven't been out in so long and then this happens.'

It was gone midnight by the time Cassie carefully let herself into the house and tiptoed up the stairs. She checked on Xander, who was sleeping peacefully, before slipping into the bathroom to change, and then carefully climbed into bed in order not to wake Joel. He was lying on his back, his breathing somewhere between heavy breathing and a light snore, and she gently poked him in the ribs to prompt him to roll over. As he obediently did so, his breathing eased so that Cassie could no longer hear it.

She sighed gently as she lay next to her husband, going over in her head all the events of the evening. After she and Sara had explained everything they knew from their sessions about the woman and where she lived, and the fact that Cassie knew the title 'Magus' was correct, Alice was able to give them lots of information about those times. She had explained that Magi would be prominent people in their communities, helping with all the necessary life ceremonies including birth, marriage, and death. From the description of the place where she lived, and especially the red rock, Alice had guessed that it was probably around the city of Petra in Jordan. Alice had also gone on to explain that Petra contained many tombs, that the Nabatean people had indeed had a strong relationship with their dead, and how their souls were sent on their way.

Cassie now lay awake, allowing all the information she had received that evening to circle inside her head for a while, and allowing it to form a picture of this woman and her home. Eventually, unable to sleep, she got back out of bed and made her way down to the kitchen to make a hot drink and collect her unicorn journal. For the next hour, she scribbled down all the information that was swimming around in her head onto the pages of her notebook. By getting it down on paper, Cassie felt as if she created space in her head so that further information and insights could come to her, and she could gain some clarity. As she paused, taking a sip of sweet camomile tea, she mused over the thought that the Magus was her. That they shared the same soul essence. That would explain the strong feeling of familiarity between them and the fact that, following her sessions with Sara, she had become hooked on all things energetic and spiritual. She had found herself reading as much as she could, absorbing as much information as possible. The sessions had triggered a fascination in her, and it had made her feel alive for the first time since Xander had been born. In fact, as she thought about it, she realised that she had never felt this alive. Her sessions with Sara had seemed to draw her out of the postnatal fog that had engulfed her, and she had found herself feeling refreshed and energised. That feeling had intensified over the last few months and she was less dependent on Joel these days, finding her confidence in speaking on the phone, looking after Xander, and generally organising her and her family's lives again. Everyone had noticed – whether they had said anything or not – how Cassie had seemed to be stepping into her power as a woman, a mother, and a wife again. It was not that she became the woman that she had been before, but that she became more than that woman. She appeared to grow and expand in some way.

It had been quite a journey, she thought, twiddling her pen in her fingers and smiling to herself. She felt so much better these days, and she was sure that the Magus was part of that recovery in some way. It was as if the Magus was sending her strong healing vibes across the Universe, willing her to find her power and become who she was meant to be.

Maybe the red hair is misleading me? she thought. The fact that the woman had red hair and that her husband's colleague, Ava, also had similar red hair confused Cassie. If they were the same woman then she knew she wouldn't feel this way towards the Magus. She frowned slightly. This woman was not Ava – who Cassie had found nice and polite but cold in some way. There had been an edge, although she couldn't put her finger on why.

No, they are definitely not the same person, Cassie said to herself, gently shaking her head. So why the red hair? She sat sipping her tea and mulling over the question in her mind.

Was the Magus drawing her attention to it in some way? Was

she highlighting this hair to catch her attention? If so, why? Why did she have to be aware of it? Why was it important? Cassie wrote these questions down in her journal, but no immediate answers were coming to her, so she put the journal carefully away and went to bed.

Cassie crept under the covers as quietly as she could. Joel did not even stir as she settled down ready for sleep. This time she dreamt heavily and vividly. She was in an underground cave of some sort, the surrounding walls rough and hewn from real strata. It was dark except for a pillar of daylight streaming in through an opening in the roof above. As Cassie moved forward, she could hear water trickling, and looking down she could see that there was a natural spring flowing over the darkened rocks on the cave floor. She was surprised to see the Magus washing herself in the freshwater stream, her tanned skin seeming to glow as she stood wet and naked on the edge of the stream of light, droplets of water making patterns on her skin. As she watched, the Magus slowly stepped into the light, holding her arms up as if to exalt some hidden deity. Her wet copper tresses hung in gentle waves down her straight back as she lifted her eyes upwards and began to chant gently into the light. The repetitive sound lulled Cassie even deeper, and the scene was lost to her as she sank into a dreamless state.

'I'm off!' Joel shouted up the stairs. 'Cassie, you awake? I'm going now.'

'Yes, I'm awake,' Cassie shouted back, a little aggravated at being woken so suddenly, and almost immediately heard the front door slam. Joel left early these days and Cassie slowly brought herself fully into the room, rubbing her eyes and stretching. She glanced at the silent baby monitor, the white light flickering slightly, and she hoped for a few minutes to herself to just wake up slowly. She turned onto her back as she slowly came back up from the deep sleep she had experienced, and as she did the imagery of her dream came back to her. As she reviewed what she had seen, she realised that there had been something else flickering on the edge of her eye line. Something that she had ignored whilst she took in as much as she could, but now it was pushing its way to the forefront of her brain. She lay in silence with her eyes closed, just allowing the imagery to wash over her again, and suddenly realised it had been a bird. It had been sitting on a rock perch, and every now and again had flapped its wings gently as if watching and taking it all in as well. She realised it was a crow and immediately the image of the crow at Sara's house came back to her. What that meant she had no idea, but she had come to realise that there were no coincidences, just breadcrumbs of information which she needed to follow.

Luckily, she had almost an hour as Xander seemed to be in a deep comfortable sleep. In his usual spreadeagle position, his dark curls framing his face beautifully, he looked so at peace. There's nothing more beautiful than a peacefully sleeping baby, Cassie thought as she tiptoed downstairs.

She quietly tidied the kitchen, washing up a few dishes which had been left on the side, and made herself a real coffee. Taking her favourite seat in the old-fashioned wicker chair in the corner, she tucked her feet under her and read through her notes from the night before. Nothing had come to her about the red hair connection and Cassie knew that if she thought about it endlessly it would just evade her. She needed to step back and give her mind some space. Eventually, the answer would reveal itself.

Cassie decided to have a shower while she had the chance and quickly and efficiently showered, dressed, and prepared herself for the day. Unbelievably, Xander slept on. Determined to use the time that was being presented to her, Cassie busied herself tidying the house. She collected some dirty clothes dumped in various rooms, and prepared a few wash piles, putting one on immediately. She then tidied the sitting room, plumping up the cushions and wiping down the coffee table. As she busied herself, her gaze took in the cabinet to one side of the fireplace, and she started to spritz and clean the glass door. She didn't need to dust inside she thought, as she peered at the collection, everything looked clean and sparkly. As her gaze took in the items displayed in neat lines, she realised that there was an extra object.

Cassie gently opened the cabinet door and peered closer trying to work out what was new. Suddenly she saw the little knife that Joel had placed on the back of the shelf and instantly recognised the symbol displayed on the sheath. Two triangles and a wavy line. She gasped and stepped back, a cold shiver causing her whole body to shake. She felt the hot prick of tears behind her eyes and a lump developed in her throat. Why on earth was she so upset? She questioned herself. She didn't stop to examine the knife further though as she could suddenly hear Xander stirring and quickly escaped the room to deal with him.

Once Xander had been changed and given a drink, Cassie placed him in his baby walker. She lay some cucumber cubes on the tray in front of him to entertain him for a while whilst she faced the cabinet. She gently wiped her sweating palms down her jeans. Her heartbeat was fast and she felt a little faint. She just couldn't understand her emotional reaction to a small trinket her husband had obviously recently bought and added to his collection. Why was it upsetting her so much? As she stood there questioning herself, the answer came to her. She was shocked by it, so much so that she initially refused to even accept it. 'No!' she said out loud, shaking her head from side to side. She began to laugh at the ludicrous idea, still shaking her head, and Xander stared up at her with a big smile slowly spreading across his face. Cassie looked down at her son's happy face and she began to laugh even more, the two of them caught in a perpetual stream of giggles. Eventually, her amusement began to fade and Xander became distracted by the light patterns streaming through the window.

Cassie looked again at the cabinet, this time with a frown developing across her face. She knew that the answer given to her was right but it both shocked and surprised her. Somehow, she had recognised the knife as the one from her past life. Why would Joel want to hurt her? Kill her even! A cold sweat began to develop across her top lip, and she wiped the droplets away with the sleeve of her jumper. The knife that Joel had brought into their home looked exactly like the one that her brother had used to stab her in that other life. The symbols were the same as those on the tiles, the symbol that she now believed meant heaven and earth. As above so below. The symbol that the Magus seemed to be connected to as well with her work with the dead. The brother who had tried to kill her in that other life was now Joel, and she was now his wife and not his sister. Did that mean that he would try and kill her in this lifetime? Were time and events repeating themselves? What had Sara said to her about events repeating when the lessons involved were not learnt, and it was decided that the lesson needed to be repeated or experienced from a slightly different perspective?

Cassie realised with a start that she needed to have a further session with Sara about this Roman life she had seen. She needed to understand what had happened, and what lesson she was supposed to be learning. In that way, she could perhaps work out whether that lesson was repeating, whether Joel was going to kill or hurt her in some way. If she could get an understanding of the commonalities between the two, then maybe she could manipulate her current life. Maybe she could rewrite it somehow and ensure that there was a happy ending this time. Her hand went to her stomach in an act of comfort, her mind rerunning the scene of her previous death. The blade sticking into her stomach and the dark red pool of blood spreading quickly across the terracotta tile and slowly enveloping the symbol. Cassie glanced at her son, a little finger of fear slowly beginning to poke at her, but she pushed it away. The face of the Magus came into her mind with her defiant black eyes staring straight at her, almost willing Cassie to be strong and to fight back. Cassie felt as if the Magus was sending her courage across the wide expanse of Universe that separated them. Sara had told her that all past, present, and future lives were happening simultaneously – which Cassie had struggled to get her head around at first. But if that were true, then the Magus was a living, breathing woman in some dimension or other, they both were, and she was sending Cassie power, strength and even advice. In fact, the Magus was sending her a warning, a warning about somebody with red hair. With a start, Cassie understood. Of course! The reference to red hair was a warning about somebody with red hair. That's why Ava's red hair seemed to have a life of its own. Ava was important and Cassie felt her stomach knot, and she doubled over slightly. Again, she put her hand to her stomach in a further act of comfort. Joel was having an affair with Ava. The realisation was painful and yet, as the thought came to her, Cassie saw in her mind's eye all those shared glances, why Joel hadn't wanted her at the company event and, no doubt, why he kept disappearing at all hours. Cassie's knees suddenly felt weak, and she sank onto the sofa, the tears beginning to flow down her cheeks. She looked at her son and her tears flowed freely. How could he do this to us? she almost screamed in her head. How?

Cassie would have stayed sobbing on the sofa for hours had it not been for Xander – who quickly became bored stuck in his baby walker and wanted to be fed and watered again. Cassie knew that she had to keep going and had to look after him for today. Once he was drifting off to sleep later that evening, she could have some time to herself to work out what she was going to do. Cassie worked her way through the necessary tasks, her tears ever ready and just below the surface, and her head seemingly full of cotton wool. She just couldn't get her thoughts straight and couldn't make sense of it all through her shock and pain. She eventually stopped trying and focused on Xander, feeding him, playing with him, and eventually bathing him before putting on a freshly washed sleep suit and settling him down to sleep. He was such an easy baby, she thought, as he quickly drifted off to sleep, a slight smile on his face.

Cassie made her way downstairs, placing the baby monitor on the side. She could see from her phone that Joel had texted her that he was going to be late home, and not to wait up for him. She stared at the message, feeling anger at the realisation that he was probably with Ava, as well as relief that she would have some time to herself tonight and she could decide what she wanted, before having to face him.

Cassie wasn't hungry. She had lost quite a bit of weight since she had started this journey, partly because she was still feeding Xander, and partly because she was so fascinated with what had been happening around her that her interest in food as a comforter had taken a back seat. She had found some passion again for life and, naturally, her body had begun to balance itself. Cassie made herself a fresh mint tea, something which had become quite common for her these days. Ever since she had seen how she had died in that past life, with a stab wound to the stomach, she had experienced physical discomfort in that area. It had always been there to some degree, but the sessions had seemingly made the symptoms worse and that had also meant that she was eating less.

Cassie took out her unicorn journal, filling the next few pages with the events and conclusions of the day, and decided she would have another session with Sara and see what further information she would gleam. Maybe that would help her to decide what she was going to do next. She reached for her phone, texted Sara for a date, and sat back in her chair waiting for a response. It took only a few seconds for Sara to respond and a time and date were quickly set.

Cassie pondered whether to tell Sara what she had found out, but since she had no real proof, she concluded that she would keep this revelation to herself for now.

The Retreat

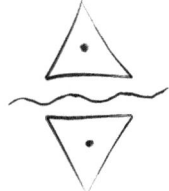

Hinat was bereft at the loss of her beloved father. From being told of his illness, to his actual passing, had been incredibly quick and Hinat felt as if she hadn't had time to take a breath and fully accept what was happening. Once he had died, there was so much to organise, and she had been busy every day making sure that the ceremony to celebrate his soul's departure was unique and truly fitting to a Priest of their temple and, of course, to a much-loved father. The whole family had helped, including Hagru – who Hinat was incredibly impressed by. Hagru had kept the house clean, organised and running beautifully without asking Hinat a single question, meaning Hinat had much-needed space to fulfil all her other commitments. Hagru had really excelled and Hinat made a mental note to let her know how pleased she was with her work. The family had also received a note from the King offering his condolences and advising them of his appreciation for the work her father had done over the years, and his immense sadness at the loss of one of his most esteemed priests. It was a moment of pride for Hinat and her family.

Since her father's departure, Hinat had also taken over his duties at the temple, assisted by the other temple workers, but primarily in charge of ensuring that the necessary duties were undertaken promptly and correctly.

Strabo's body had been washed and loosely wrapped in a beautiful blue cloak heavily adorned with crystal, depicting his valuable work in the temple, before being carried to a sky platform especially reserved for dignitaries. His sons, Hinat's brothers, had carried him to his final resting place but Hinat had been unable to go with them. She could not bear to watch, her grief washing over her in giant waves which she could just not control, and which threatened to completely drown her in emotion. A couple of the other workers kindly volunteered to go in her place when they saw how distressed she was. They carefully arranged Strabo's naked body, laying him on his beautifully adorned cloak on the platform, and arranging the crystals and perfume bottles around him as Hinat had instructed, while her brothers stood back to chant, burn incense and pray for his soul's protection and swift transition. As the sun set, causing darkness to descend within a few minutes, the little party slowly made their way back to the temple. Hinat watched from afar, the flames of their torches only visible to her as a moving line of light in the darkness, as they made their way home. Her heart was so heavy that it physically hurt, and she could not stop the stream of tears from escaping. The wetness of her face was highlighted by the hand torch she held as she waited for the small band of figures to return.

The following weeks were a blur for Hinat. She knew the time would come when she would need to collect her father's bones, but each time she thought of it, the grief descended – paralysing and enveloping her again. She tried to push it to the back of her mind, to keep herself busy, but it was exhausting not to honour her emotions and allow the grief to show.

Eventually, one of her brothers suggested that she take time for a retreat. Hinat had not thought to do this during her heightened emotions, but once it was suggested, it seemed to be an obvious and helpful idea. Hinat would go into the desert for several days on her own, to sleep, contemplate, and commune with Spirit. These retreats were often taken in times of extreme emotion, giving space to heal and find a way forward.

Hagru helped to pack several bags of supplies for Hinat, and her brothers carried all the items that she would need, as they made their way into the desert to find a spot where she could make camp. It was several hours away from the city, at the base of an enormous red outcrop, sheltered by an array of huge rocks which had fallen from the cliffs over the years, and which now provided a natural enclave and, most importantly, essential shade. It was a safe and cool space, secluded and quiet. It was perfect for the task at hand. As the small group made their way into the centre of the rocks, Hinat saw several patches of irises growing up from the sandy soil. They were the black irises commonly found around Raqmu, and they seemed to greet her to this space of healing with their heavy scent. It was a good omen.

Hinat waved at the tiny figures on the horizon as her brothers, having helped her to set up camp, slowly made their way home in the heat of the day. She squinted at the fierce sun as she drew her headscarf further forward over her face and retreated to the shade of the rocks. She suddenly felt very alone and vulnerable but knew that she needed to speak to Spirit about everything that was troubling her.

Hinat unwrapped her headscarf from around her head and placed it on the ground by the side of the makeshift mattress. She would need it later. There was a rug on the floor, keeping most of the dirt and dust at bay, and several small oil lamps scattered about. Her supplies of food and water were stacked at the back of the tent in one corner, the space marked out with a line of stones, and some twine had been hung across the ceiling of the tent so that she had somewhere to hang her clothes. Hinat had set up several bowls of frankincense resin. She could not imagine communing with Spirit without it, and she took a deep breath as the heady scent filled the tent. Hinat's eyes scanned the space with gratitude for the way her brothers had carried so many items and set up her retreat so lovingly for her. Her heart swelled with the love and support that they were showing her when she needed them most. She knew that they were also struggling with grief but, somehow, they seemed to be coping better. Probably because of their wives and children, Hinat thought. She was not coping well, and she knew that this retreat was necessary for her survival.

Hinat lay down on the mattress set out on one side of the tent, closing her eyes, and allowing her mind to settle and relax. It took some time as her thoughts were racing, and the grief had so exhausted her that her head hurt as the tension of the last few weeks began the process of seeping away. As her body followed suit and relaxed, Hinat felt all sorts of aches and pains and realised that her whole body had been tense and her muscles tight. As they let go of the tension, physical pain was released as well as several waves of emotion seemingly in succession. A wave of anger swept through her first and Hinat could have ripped the tent apart with her bare hands. She lay there clenching and unclenching her fists as she recognised the emotion but with a great effort allowed it to just dissipate without reacting to it. A wave of deep sadness followed for the end of a chapter with her father as the head of the family, his presence and support now sorely missed. A wave of disappointment with Spirit that this had to happen in this life she was living, and such a wave of love that her body shook, and the tears fell again. Eventually, the waves stopped coming and Hinat felt a deep and peaceful relaxation for the first time in weeks. She allowed herself to savour this for a while, before gently falling into a restful sleep.

Hinat woke in the pitch black, shivering slightly. She had not intended to sleep so long and had not covered herself in the afternoon heat, but as darkness had fallen the temperature had also dropped, and she was now cold. She slowly turned over on her side and, although she was shivering, she allowed her eyes to slowly adjust to the darkness before carefully getting up from the mattress. There was a pile of covers and blankets near her feet and she found a couple, placing them over her now dishevelled bedding for later. She quickly wrapped a shawl around her shoulders and hugged it to her. One of the bowls of frankincense was still smouldering, a faint ember illuminating the tent. Hinat made her way carefully to the supplies corner by the dim light and found her jar of flints. With expertise, she was able to quickly start a fire in a crater dug on the other side of the tent, away from the rug and mattress. One of her brothers had lined and edged it with small stones, which were perfect for warming dishes and lightly cooking some items when a fire was eventually roaring and heating them through. He had set up some basic kindling, so it was ready to light, and Hinat quickly had a fire going. The flames cast weird shadows over the walls of the tent, which seemed to dance and sway in the glow. Hinat found a pouch which one of her sister-in-law's had prepared with her supper for the night and tucked in heartily. The relaxation and deep sleep had made her hungry and she ate everything that had been prepared for her, washing it down with some water brought with her in several animal skin pouches. There was enough for four days, and her brothers would be back to collect her once the time had elapsed. Hinat knew that she needed to make the most of her solitude and gain as much insight as possible into her situation. Why had her father had to pass at this time, and what did that mean for her going forward? She carefully tidied up, not wanting to attract any vermin, and made her way outside behind the rear corner of the tent, where a second, deeper hole had been dug and edged with stones for her ablutions. When she was ready to leave, she would easily infill this hole, ensuring that nothing was left unburied.

Making her way back to her bed, Hinat snuggled down into the covers and easily drifted back to sleep. In her dream, Hinat could see herself crouching by a narrow stream of shallow water, as it gently flowed over a huge flat rock. She was naked and splashing the water carefully over her body, causing the droplets to be seemingly highlighted in a light coming from above. As she looked around, she could see that it was a cave, the edges dark and ominous in her peripheral vision, but there was enough light to see. Hinat couldn't quite make out where it was coming from, but it was above her as it danced and highlighted the copper of her hair. Eventually, she was able to look upwards and could see that the light was flooding through a hole in the roof of the cave, casting a spotlight on the floor below. She wondered what she was doing there and where this cave was, but nothing instantly came to her. Hinat thought she could see a bird but she wasn't sure if it was the shadows playing tricks on her. Eventually, the scene faded as she sank deeper into a dreamless sleep again.

Hinat woke gently the next morning. She very slowly became aware of her surroundings. It took great effort to open her eyes, and she took in the interior of the tent, remembering where she was. She lay very still, listening to the early morning sounds of the desert, and realised that she didn't need to move or go anywhere this morning. The day was her own and she could sleep through it all if she wanted to. The thought made her smile and relax, and she slowly closed her eyes again.

This time she dreamt of the cave again, but she was not alone. There was a tall young man with her, with dark curly hair. She couldn't see his face as he had his back to her, but she could tell that he was slender and had to stoop to avoid banging his head on the roof of the cave. Several of the curls on his head seemed to be highlighted in the light and she took some time studying the shape and size of the individual curls, as if they were out of proportion somehow. When he eventually turned his head towards her, there were no facial features there, only a blank white space. Hinat stepped back in shock and, as she did so, he bent forward and handed her a bundle. Still slightly taken aback, she looked down and realised that she was holding a baby, and it was crying loudly. The noise seemed to get louder and louder and eventually penetrated the darkest corners of her mind as it echoed and bounced around the inside of her head.

Hinat opened her eyes and could feel that the tent was heating up. She was thirsty now and, throwing the covers off, she made her way to the water pouches, the noise of the baby still in her ears. As she took a satisfying drink, she realised that the noise was no longer in her head but was coming from outside. Hinat carefully opened the door of the tent, rolling back the fabric and tying it in place, before breathing in the fresh air and peering out to find the source of the cries. Scratching around in the earth, in the shade of one of the huge fallen rocks, were three, large, black birds, noisily chatting to each other as they searched for some scraps to eat. As they did so, they performed a sort of dance, circling each other and flapping their wings in a mesmerising flowing action. Hinat realised this was the noise that she had been hearing as she woke from her dream. She shook her head slightly trying to make sense of the fact that the dream sounds seemed to merge into a different reality without any obvious break. Slowly, as she awoke more fully, the noise in her head vanished and she was able to take in the view of her retreat surroundings. The sun was already warming up the scene and she could immediately feel the impending heat. It was going to be a scorching day and Hinat was grateful that her tent was permanently in the shadow of the huge red rocks around her.

The landscape was barren, but still alive and brimming with colour. There were the dark sprinkles of black iris flowers and green foliage against the red scorched sand, and the huge red rocks, merging into stripes of purple in the darker shade. When Hinat turned her head upwards, the sky was a vibrant intense blue, and every so often she could see the black birds, always highlighted against whatever backdrop they had found. She felt protected and safe in this familiar landscape now that she had slept so deeply. She knew it so well, the colours, the smells, and the sounds. It was part of her, part of her father and her ancestors. Hinat realised that she had thought about her father without crying for the first time, and she felt relieved and guilty all at the same time. She turned back into the tent to wash and change her clothes, before making a hot cup of char and eating some dates she found in another pouch. Sitting with her back against one of the huge rocks which had tumbled from the cliff many years ago, she felt contented and realised that she had needed this space so badly – to reconnect with what was important in her life. She felt a wave of gratitude wash over her for the amazing familial love she was experiencing, and for her father, who had not only loved her and her brothers but nurtured and protected them. Her eyes stung slightly as she felt the tears looming, and disappointed in their presence again, she blinked them away. She didn't want to grieve or cry anymore. She was tired of being sad. She realised that she wanted to live again fully and to make her father and family proud. Hinat wanted to celebrate how lucky she had been, and as these thoughts emerged and formed, Hinat felt herself smile in relief.

Under the watchful gaze of the three black birds, who seemed to want to keep Hinat company and had found a perch overlooking her tent, Hinat pulled her mattress outside and set a bowl of frankincense resin at each corner. She then carefully arranged several lines of crystals in patterns fanning out from the centre. She gently prepared herself physically by washing her face and adorning herself with some perfume which her father had gifted her some time previously. She wanted to set the intention that it was her father who visited her, or at least that she received information about him, and the best way was to bring into the energy something that had been his, or which he had gifted her with love. As she settled down on the makeshift bed, in the shadows of a fierce desert sun, she smiled at the unusual scene and shook her head slightly. It was such a strange setting for her meeting with Spirit, but also extremely serene and beautiful. She gazed up at the three birds, all staring at her intently, as if they couldn't quite make out what this strange human was doing but were slightly amused at her behaviour, nevertheless. They screeched at her several times, as if laughing and mocking her, but stayed put on their perch.

'You better be quiet you three, I need a bit of peace for this,' Hinat told them. 'Don't be disturbing me or there will be trouble.'

The three birds flapped their wings and then settled down, tucking themselves into a seated position as if they had heard and understood her and couldn't wait to see what was about to happen. Hinat smiled at them. 'I didn't think I was going to have an audience!' she said out loud to herself and the birds, chuckling slightly. Hinat wrapped her headscarf around her eyes to keep out the light of the day and settled down in readiness.

Slowly, Hinat instructed her body to relax, allowing her mind to drift down into a trance-like state. As she did so, Hinat set an intention to speak to Spirit and to gain the clarity that she required. Eventually, as she descended along her familiar route, her mind slowed sufficiently for her Soul essence to step out and into a safe space to have that conversation.

As Hinat stepped into the circle of light, she felt excited and eager to see what was going to happen. She stood for some time, bathed in the sparkling white light that now surrounded and held her before a strange man stepped forward. She didn't recognise him but could feel his presence and instantly felt as if he was a guide, benevolent and kind. He was dressed in a long blue robe, with a strange-shaped high headdress. She knew that he was a priest but was not of this lifetime. She recognised his energy but just couldn't put her finger on who he was, if anyone, in her current life. As they stood face to face in the circle of light, he smiled at her as if encouraging her to ask a question.

'Is my father okay?' Hinat eventually asked.

'He has returned to Source and to the light. He is well and has learnt a lot in this lifetime. He has accomplished most of what he set out to do and has passed on his knowledge to you, my dear. You are protected and safe but must search for your own purpose.'

Hinat was intrigued at this response. 'What is my purpose?'

The priest smiled at her. 'That is for you to find out, but know that in finding all parts of yourself, you will also find your purpose.'

'All parts of myself? Have I lost some parts? Are there more than just me?' The questions came out in a rush as Hinat tried to make sense of what she was hearing.

'Absolutely. Your Soul has lived in many lifetimes and places, and you will have left some energy in all those parts. Some of those parts may struggle at times and you will feel that. Some may even need your assistance if they are not to be lost and cause harm to the whole.'

Hinat was quiet for a while as she took in all this information. She didn't want to waste her questions, so thought carefully before asking, 'Is a part struggling at the moment?'

The priest nodded but did not speak.

'How is it struggling?' Hinat asked.

'You must find your way to connect and discover what you need to know to restore equilibrium, otherwise, you will repeat the same lesson again and again.'

Hinat felt a slight panic arising but tried to relax and stay calm. She didn't want to repeat anything, it just seemed like such a waste of time.

'How do I connect?' she asked. Almost as she asked the question, she was shown the cave again. The cave with the faceless man and the crying baby. This must be important, Hinat thought, noting the information for later recall. As she continued to take in the scene in front of her, she could see herself standing in the pool of light, her naked body glistening and her arms stretched upwards as if in worship. She couldn't hear anything but knew that she was connecting with someone across time and space. As she continued to watch, the cave morphed into one of beautiful pale blue crystals glinting in the sparkling light. Eventually, the image faded, and the priest reappeared.

Hinat decided not to ask questions about the cave – it was clearly going to be revealed to her – so she asked, 'Why is the part struggling?'

'The part has been weakened and the lesson has not been

learnt. Sometimes we take on too many lessons for one lifetime and our energy is depleted. This is one such time. You believed you could do this, and you can, but you need more energy to be successful. You need more parts to help. If you are not successful this time, there will be repercussions,' the priest offered.

Hinat nodded with concern. She didn't like the sound of that, as if she would be going backwards somehow in her Soul growth. She didn't feel as if the priest was going to give her much more information now though. It was obviously something she had to find out for herself. She smiled at him. 'Thank you for your help,' she said. 'Please tell my father that I love and miss him and am so grateful that he was in my life.'

The priest smiled at her, and from behind him, stepped her father. Hinat rushed into her father's arms, desperate to feel his embrace and connect with his energy again. He soothed and hugged her for some time, whispering gently in her ear, before disentangling himself and stepping back.

'Goodbye, my darling. Know that I am always here supporting and guiding you. Know that it is now your time to shine and show your true power. You are far more powerful than I, Hinat, if only you believed. I love you.'

It must have been over an hour before Hinat was ready to come back into her physical body. She slowly became aware of her surroundings, feeling the air on her skin, and tuning into the earth sounds, before gently opening her eyes. She remained on the mattress for some time even though she was back in the present, just mulling over the information that had been given to her and relishing the rest she felt it had given her mind, body, and soul. She was humbled by the task that was in front of her, and slightly startled by what she had been shown. However, if Spirit believed she could do it, then she was obviously capable and would do her best to achieve what all parts of her Soul needed. She could see her father in her mind's eye and could feel the pride flowing from him. This spurred Hinat on even more and filled her with a knowing, realising that her father was always with her. He really hadn't gone far., Although physically she would no longer be able to see him, energetically she was aware of his presence close to her, and Hinat felt comforted and happy with this situation. Hinat gently unwrapped the headscarf from her eyes, blinking in the light. As she looked around her the three black birds had moved from their perch and appeared to be in a circle around her. Hinat looked at them all in turn and they returned her stare. She realised that they were significant and may be here to support and protect her.

As Hinat cooked and ate her supper that night, she devised some more questions for Spirit. She wasn't sure that the priest would give her the information that she needed, but it was worth asking and she didn't want to miss this opportunity. As she mulled over the information she had been given, the baby appeared to her repeatedly. Is this a real baby or does it represent a new beginning? Hinat couldn't make up her mind, although, as she had no partner, a new beginning seemed more likely. She knew that time would reveal the truth of the message.

Hinat continued to commune with Spirit as many times as she could over the few days that she had before her brothers came to collect her. She returned from the retreat feeling refreshed, rested and a lot happier. She knew that her path had been planned and would be revealed to her and that her father was right by her side. His presence gave her certainty that she could fulfil the task given to her by Spirit.

Hinat was pregnant. She knew without a single doubt that she was carrying a baby and that she would be a mother soon. She was sitting on her bedroom floor after a long day at the temple. Hagru had prepared a simple but delicious supper on her return, and whilst Hagru washed the dishes and tidied the kitchen, Hinat readied herself for bed. These days she was tired to the bone most nights. She knew why, of course, but she also knew that the ones closest to her were concerned with her fatigue. She was aware that she would need to tell them soon that she was expecting her first child and was sure that they would be supportive and excited for her. In their society, women were extremely important and revered for the fact that they could bring forth new life. It did not matter what circumstances they may find themselves in, the community would be supportive and rally around them. Each child was important to their ancestors, carrying on the traditions and ideals of their culture.

Finding out about her pregnancy had been a surprise, even though Spirit had shown it to her at the Retreat. Hinat had convinced herself that the baby represented a new beginning which seemed more apt at the time, but this baby was definitely real.

Hinat rubbed the oil gently across her slightly swollen belly, enjoying the quiet time and closeness with her baby. The father, Omar, worked in the purple temple with her friend Gamilat, and it was through her that Hinat had first met him. As soon as she had set eyes on him, Hinat had remembered the dream of a dark curly-haired man, tall and slender but faceless, and handing her a baby. He was indeed tall and handsome, with the tight curly black hair she had seen, as well as beautiful brown eyes that you could almost drown in. His face easily lit up with the biggest, brightest smile you could imagine. Omar was fun, always teasing and laughing, and his energy was bright and strong. He had the most amazing gift of sight, being able to see many past lives of an individual almost simultaneously just by being in their presence. From the information he gained through these Soul windows, he was able to direct individuals to the lesson that needed to be learnt in the current lifetime, so they could grasp the learning and not be destined to keep repeating it. Through his work, Omar helped others to evolve and expand their energy in a way that pushed them forward more quickly to their life purpose and destiny. Omar was famed for his work and was often sought out by dignitaries for information on their future as a country and a people. Hinat had immediately been drawn to him, not only because of the dream but also because the work he did was exactly what she needed to learn, to fulfil her purpose according to the priest.

Gamilat had introduced them at an open evening at the temple and Hinat had been intrigued.

'Omar, this is my good friend, Hinat. She's the head priestess at the blue temple.'

'Hi Hinat,' Omar smiled broadly, and his eyes twinkled. 'I've heard about the amazing things you have been doing at your temple. It's different and original.'

'Thank you that's really kind. I've heard of your work as well, of course. I might need your help, to be honest.'

'That sounds interesting. Come and sit with me and tell me what you need to know,' Omar replied and ushered Hinat to a private corner to chat. Hinat found it so easy to tell Omar about her father, her grief and her need to discover her purpose in life. He was attentive and interested in what she had to say, and they had chatted most of the evening. Eventually, he walked her home, gently touching her hand as they parted. Hinat had felt such a jolt of recognition with the unexpected touch, and she knew that they were destined to be together. Omar did too, and their relationship had been passionate and exciting. However, Omar was not ready to be tied down to Hinat and their child, and she was aware of this. She had always been aware that he had his own purpose, and that – for now – they were not destined to be a family. They both knew that they would always have a connection, and maybe they would come back together when they had both matured, but at this time, Omar was too focused on his career and what he wanted to achieve.

Omar was dedicated to expanding his gift to its limit, and to do so he needed to be extremely disciplined – ensuring that his physical body was in top condition, his mind was in the best shape it could be, and his devotion to Spirit was strong. Hinat knew that he would be supportive of her, and be around for their child, but whether they would decide to create a family group, she did not know. However, there was no judgement or discrimination in her community if she chose to be alone or with Omar, either was accepted and the situation was primarily a celebration of life.

Hinat always thought of her father when she connected to the baby, and she knew that he was aware of this new addition to the family and may in fact have chosen this Soul to join the long line of ancestors that stretched back through time and space. Hinat knew that the baby had been chosen for a reason. She didn't know what that reason was but knew that this Soul needed to come into the world for a particular task. She also knew that she and her father had been with this Soul in a past life. That the three of them had been together before and that there were bonds of love and respect already in place.

Hinat was excited and looked forward to the day that her baby arrived. She also knew, and her friend Gamilat had confirmed it, that the baby would be a girl born into the long line of strong women that formed their lineage. Women who used their energetic skills to help others – whether that was through prophecy, health, guidance, or healing. Hinat also knew that she would call her daughter after one of the crystals that she used so often in the temple. This was something that she hadn't voiced with her family, as she wasn't sure how they would take this news, but she knew it was the right thing to do and she believed it had been confirmed to her in one of her dreams on the Retreat. The use of crystals was unique to her temple and the energy of this Soul was also unique. The two elements just seemed to fit beautifully together.

Hinat hugged her belly and giggled to herself. She was so excited about what was to come.

Matteo

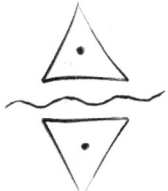

Joel sat at the breakfast bar watching his mother as she busied herself making them both a pot of tea.

'It's so lovely to see you, Joel,' she said, smiling at her son. 'I haven't seen any of you for a while. How's my favourite grandson?'

'He's your only grandson, Mum,' Joel said, pretending to be irritated. 'He's fine,' he added with a smile.

'And Cassie?' Joel looked at his mother, and his grim expression made her frown slightly. Sitting down next to him she leant towards him slightly and said, 'What's going on?'

'Nothing really. It's just that I'm not feeling myself at the moment.'

'What do you mean?' she asked, sitting back to pour them both a cup of freshly brewed tea. 'Why aren't you feeling well?'

Joel hung his head. He knew his mother would be disappointed in him and he could hardly bear the drama that was about to break out, but he knew that he needed additional help, and he also knew that his mother loved him dearly. She would help him as much as she could.

'It's my anger. I can keep it under control, but I feel as if it's expanding inside me somehow, and that it's about to blow. It's like this heavy dark energy bubbling away. I just don't know what to do.' He looked up at his mother's face and the tears stung his eyes.

'Well, I know what you should do,' she said gently but firmly as she patted his knee. 'You need to see that counsellor I found for you. The one who specialises in anger. I've heard he is good and gets excellent results. You need more outside help now, Joel, this has gone far enough. I'll book you in if you like.' She looked at his face, her eyebrows raised slightly as she waited for his response.

Eventually, it came almost in a whisper. 'I'm already going for some counselling. It's helping but it feels very slow going, but I'll go and see the one you found as well.' He nodded his head slowly as if he was exhausted. He didn't mention that his father had arranged the counselling up to now, or had been taking him, he just couldn't bear any more drama.

Sophia lay on the flowered chaise longue in the corner of her conservatory, a hot mug of tea in her hand. It was her favourite place to just lie and contemplate the world. The light was so beautiful in this corner of the house, and the surrounding foliage of her beloved plants instantly calmed and soothed her. Today, however, she couldn't settle. Almost as her bottom touched the seat, she was up again pottering around the plants and finding jobs to do. She couldn't just sit still, her anxiety was through the roof worrying about Joel and his family, and she just needed to keep busy. Sophia screwed up her face slightly as she concentrated on removing the dead leaves from her largest begonia and trimming the branches slightly to ensure that it didn't get too sprawling and uneven. Joel had made her proud of late – being proactive about getting help. She knew he was really trying hard to overcome his dark episodes. Sophia had no idea where they came from, though. He seemed to be angry from the minute that he had been born, whilst she and Patrick were both fairly easygoing. However, he just didn't look well. He looked grey almost and Sophia wasn't sure whether this was because he was dealing with this emotional crisis and it was really taking a toll on him, or whether there was something else. Whenever she saw him, he looked drained and exhausted. At his age he should be bursting with energy, she thought, as she carefully watered the row of hanging plants which stretched across the central beam of the roof of the conservatory. The different tones of green and leaf shapes made a beautifully stunning living curtain, almost dividing the room into two. Sophia would often sit here just marvelling at the beauty of the foliage, one of her passions in life. Her plants and this room gave her renewed energy and purpose.

As she finally went to sit again, through the window, she saw Martha making her way slowly in the grey drizzle to her back door. Sophia instantly rose again, almost in one fluid motion, and headed to the door to let her friend in.

They sat together beneath the plant curtain with their mugs of tea. Martha's secret had been bugging her and causing her to lose sleep and she knew that she needed to be open and honest with Sophia. It was not her information to keep secret and she didn't want to change the course of the path that they were all on if it was not for her to do so. She couldn't bear it if something happened to Cassie because she hadn't delivered the message that she had been given in its entirety. She looked intently at her friend with a pained expression on her face, as she knew Sophia would be upset. However, it had to be done and Martha spent the next half an hour explaining to Sophia the full message that had been given to her, and the fact that she believed this woman to be Cassie herself in another time and space, warning herself about Joel's actions.

'I spoke to Sara and there's no reason why it's not possible. There is a belief that there is no linear time, and all our lives are happening simultaneously, so it's possible to tap into them now to gain information about a lesson that we are learning today, and to get some help if we want to change the course of events playing out. I find it amazing, and it's really made me look at my current life differently. What lessons are playing out? What, if anything, do I need to change, and how am I going to do that?' Martha hunched her shoulders and put her palms up as she said this, as if to emphasise the questions.

Sophia was silent for a minute as her friend finished talking, taking in all that she had heard and playing it in her mind. It was indeed amazing, but equally very confusing, and she found it easier to focus on parts of the problem. For Sophia, the most upsetting part was that Joel and Cassie's marriage was struggling. Sophia was cross with Joel for his behaviour, and deeply concerned that his anger would take him on a dark path. Where that fitted in the whole equation, and where that might lead them all, she didn't know, but for now, the anger was the focus point. She expressed her concerns to Martha.

'I'm so scared that his temper is going to cause something to happen that he can't take back,' she admitted. 'The fact that he is having an affair is terrible and makes me so cross with him, but his anger frightens me. I don't think for a minute that he would hurt anyone deliberately, I don't mean it like that. I just worry that his anger will be so consuming to him that he will do something that he can't control, and that will get him into trouble.

What should we do, Martha?' Sophia asked. Her eyes were moist, and her voice trembled slightly. 'How can we help them both?'

The two friends sat in silence for a while, mulling over everything they knew and trying to make sense of the extraordinary ideas and concepts that had suddenly come into their lives.

As they sipped their tea, Sophia ventured, 'Do you think you could contact that woman…' she caught herself. 'I mean, do you think we could talk to Cassie from that other life and find out how we can help?' Her eyebrows raised as she said it. 'Goodness, it's like some science fiction film or something,' she added and they both chuckled. It was a much-needed release of tension for them both.

'I don't see why not,' Martha said. 'I've been speaking to Spirit since I was a child. I suppose it's only a small step to speak to someone specifically in a different dimension,' and she shrugged her shoulders. 'We could certainly try – she did speak to me at Christmas, after all.' With that, Martha quickly explained to Sophia how the past life version of Cassie had indeed spoken to her on Christmas Day, but not since then. 'Let's meet up tomorrow evening as Roger and Patrick are going to that council meeting, and I can fully concentrate on contacting that woman again.'

'We can't call her 'that woman', and if we call her Cassie that will also be confusing. We'll have to ask her what her name is,' Sophia concluded. 'Okay let's say 7 p.m. tomorrow. We can shut the door and do it in here.'

'Okay, it's a date. I'm quite excited,' Martha stated, smiling at her friend. 'I'm not sure how this is going to pan out, but we can certainly try. Try not to worry,' she added patting her friend's shoulder in reassurance.

As soon as Cassie arrived for her next session, Sara explained that Martha had rung her for some clarification about past, present, and future lives. She had divulged no information whatsoever about their sessions but had explained to Martha that it was certainly possible to contact other lives, to step in and out of other dimensions and, in theory, there wasn't a reason why you couldn't contact yourself to try and change a recurring problem.

'That's interesting,' Cassie said. 'Those questions must have occurred to her after speaking to the Magus that day in the kitchen, when she was giving me a reading. I know the Magus was trying to warn me about Ava and now I have the binding spell to use as well.'

She looked over at Sara and started to explain the realisations that had come to her after their evening with Alice. 'I'm sure he's having an affair with his work colleague, Ava. She's got vivid red hair like the Magus. The way I've been seeing it in the sessions has made me think that it's a warning. That she's warning me about a red-haired woman, and that's why it's really highlighted. I'm not sure why the other life is coming up now, but Joel bought this knife and it has exactly the same symbol on it that I saw on the tiles.'

'Really!?' Sara exclaimed in surprise. 'The same symbol as on the tiles? That's interesting. No wonder it triggered you if that's the knife, or certainly a similar one to the one that stabbed you. But how is everything connected?'

'I have no idea but I thought we could explore the Roman life again today. See if anything else comes up. What do you think?' Cassie looked at her friend for agreement.

'Yes, sounds like a good idea,' Sara said nodding. 'What essential oil would you like me to put on?'

Cassie pondered for a moment. 'Although it's not connected yet to the Roman life let's put the elemi and myrrh on again. I love that combination and maybe it will help me in some way, especially if the two lives I've been seeing are also connected.'

'Okay,' Sara said as she busied herself setting up the diffuser and dropping in a couple of drops of each oil.

As the aroma began to filter out into the room, Cassie drew in the smell. 'It's so indicative. It just takes me into trance, like it's a trigger.'

As she uttered those words, she settled herself down on the cushions and was almost immediately back in the Roman life, with hardly any induction required. Sara was surprised but pleased that Cassie was obviously developing so quickly. She realised that everything seemed to be heightened since the Magus had come into their lives. She wondered whether the connection between Cassie and herself over time and space had somehow caused psychic energy and phenomena to be expanded and was causing unusual events to take place.

Sara drew her focus back to the session in hand, reassuring Cassie as they both set their intentions to follow the energy and discover any connection to the different lives. 'Just take your time and let me know what you can sense,' Sara offered as Cassie's eyelids began to flutter and her body relaxed even further.

'I think I'm back in the courtyard. I can feel the sun, it's a hot country that I'm in. I'm hiding again, I'm always hiding!' she sighed as she absorbed the information around her…

Ophelia peered around the pillar, her heart beating wildly. She gasped as she tried to catch her breath, but her chest felt tight, and she struggled. She sat back slightly, willing herself to calm down and for her breathing to come under control. It took several minutes for her breath to settle. The whole time her senses were on high alert, trying to hear the slightest sound and to know whether Matteo was close. Ophelia felt exhausted with the anxiety and fear that coursed through her, the struggle to breathe, and the confusion she felt about the situation. Her mind was a fog and she battled to think straight. She was not sure how long she crouched behind the pillar, cloaked in its shadow, but slowly she became aware of footsteps, and she was instantly alert. Her ears strained to decide from which direction the sound was coming, and she carefully peered around the pillar to gain sight of her pursuer. She could not believe that her brother would behave in this way. They had always been close and, since her parent's death, she had felt that they shared a stronger bond. Siblings watching over each other. However, the arrival of her new sister-in-law on the scene had changed everything. Matteo never had time for her anymore and just brushed her aside whenever she tried to speak with him. He had changed towards her. Ophelia had felt more and more alone, and it had really begun to trouble her. Matteo's new wife, Luna, was arrogant and instantly acted as if she was far superior, trying to push Ophelia around whenever possible, even though they were of a similar age. Luna clearly felt Ophelia's presence was a hindrance, and Ophelia had heard her moaning to Matteo about having to look after her now that his parents were dead, instead of enjoying their early married years alone together. Ophelia knew that Luna would have happily sent her away if there was anywhere for her to go, but with her parents gone and no relatives nearby, there was nothing Ophelia could do but bear the brunt of Luna's disdain. Ophelia knew that it was affecting her confidence and self-worth badly but there was no talking to Matteo, and she had nowhere else to turn. Her heart broke with the realisation that they wanted her gone at any cost, and that killing her was an option. With shock, she also realised that if she was dead, Matteo would inherit her parents' full estate which would last him and Luna considerably longer and make them very well off.

Ophelia held her breath as she took another peek around the pillar. Suddenly the looming shadow of Matteo holding a knife covered the rear wall of the terrace, and Ophelia stared wide-eyed at the clarity of the image. Adrenaline pumped through her body, and she backed away along the darkened wall behind her. If she could get to the back gate in the rear wall she could escape to the street outside, but after that, she had no idea where she was going to go.

Ophelia continued creeping back along the wall, her line of vision ahead of her as she waited for Matteo to emerge around the corner of the courtyard. Suddenly, she heard a very slight noise behind her. Whirling around, she came face to face with her brother. His dark curly hair was flattened to his sweaty forehead, and droplets trickled down the sides of his face and off his nose. Before Ophelia even had time to speak, Matteo plunged the knife into her stomach. She dropped instantly to her knees with the force of the action and the shock. The sound of rushing energy filled her ears and a searing pain coursed down her legs. She fell forward with a thump, pushing the knife even deeper into her body and banging her face on the cool tiles, as a dark pool of blood quickly seeped out from under her.

Matteo stood completely still as this scene played out in front of him. His eyes were wide with the shock of his actions, and the speed of their effect on his sister. Almost immediately, a wave of regret and shame coursed over him, and he dropped to her side, gently repeating her name as the trickles of sweat mixed with his tears. What had he done? Why had he listened to Luna? Surely, they could all have lived and thrived together? His mind raced with questions, accusations, and the fear of the repercussions that were going to come crashing down on him. He watched as the blood pooled even further around the body of his young sister, slowly covering the symbol of his family's beliefs and morals in a stunningly vivid paradox.

Sara's voice slowly filtered into Cassie's brain, and she expertly took her beyond the point of death and into the spirit world, where she could find forgiveness for her brother and work through the emotions and thoughts that she had passed over with.

'Tell me, is your Guide still with you?' Sara asked.

'Yes, she's here,' Cassie slowly replied. Her voice low and soft.

'Can you ask her what the connection is between this life and the Magus?'

There was a long pause as Cassie allowed the information to seep into her understanding. She had no concept of time in this state of trance but floated in the highly relaxed state until an awareness slowly filtered into her conscious mind.

'The Magus is me. I don't want anyone to ever take advantage of me again. I have suffered as a woman over the years in many lifetimes and have also been the perpetrator of unkind deeds to women as well. I have been learning from all perspectives and I know that this cycle must now stop. I must step into my full power and now is the time.'

There was silence while Cassie listened again, and Sara felt as if she was almost channelling the information and advice from her guide.

'I can see a long line of women standing behind me. I have seen this before – as if all the women I have been in many lifetimes are supporting me and willing me to break this cycle. There is a thread that runs through my whole Soul Continuum that is about learning to step into my own power, and I have not always managed it. As the Magus, I did step into my power and was a force to be reckoned with. I felt so strong in that lifetime, and as I connect to her, I feel that strength, that energy seeping into my physical body now. That sounds weird but it's how I feel.'

'It's not weird,' Sara reassured her. 'There's no wrong or right way. If it resonates with you then I'm sure it is what is right for you.'

Cassie frowned slightly and tilted her head as if she was listening intently to an unseen figure. Sara waited and watched patiently.

'I think the Magus is doing something to Joel,' Cassie eventually stated.

'What do you mean?' Sara asked.

'Well, she's sending me energy for strength and empowerment, and I can see it like a stream of light full of the little symbols she uses on her face, streaming into my energy field. But I can also see the same going to Joel, but it feels darker somehow. I'm not sure what she's – what I'm – doing,' she corrected herself.

After a further pause, Cassie concluded that she just couldn't get the meaning of what was happening to Joel, but she had an uneasy feeling about it.

Before ending the session completely, Sara took Cassie to a space where she could meet Matteo and have a conversation with him about why he had betrayed her. Sara wanted Cassie to see if she could forgive him for his actions in that lifetime, as that was the key to releasing any negative energy that Cassie was holding in her energy field, connected to that life. It took a while, but eventually, Cassie felt that she could offer true forgiveness, and Matteo dropped to his knees in her mind's eye, sobbing gently. Cassie could feel that he was genuinely remorseful, and she knew that by sending Matteo forgiveness across time and space, she was also offering Joel forgiveness on some level. Cassie hoped that by offering forgiveness to Matteo, he would release any anger that he held and which he had obviously brought into this life as Joel. 'Do you think we can help him release the anger that he holds?' she asked Sara.

Sara paused for a while, thinking through the situation,

before she said, 'Why don't you ask your Guide what we can do to help?'

'Okay,' Cassie said. There was a long pause as Cassie conversed silently with her Guide, and Sara held space while watching Cassie's gentle breathing. 'She says to take him back to the root of the problem. What does that mean? Is that possible?' Cassie's forehead knitted slightly.

'Well, let's try. Let's set our intention to see the root of Matteo's anger and see what happens. Just focus back on your breath and allow it to soften even more.' Sara watched Cassie as she deepened even further into a relaxed state. 'When you are ready, let's ask to see the root of Matteo's anger'.

Cassie nodded slightly but didn't speak or open her eyes, remaining lying on the soft pile of cushions, breathing gently.

Sara waited, closing her eyes as well and allowing her breathing to relax and soften as she held space for Cassie and waited for her to speak.

Eventually, Cassie began to describe what she was seeing. 'I am being shown a woman. She is dressed in long, rough robes, with a shawl over her head. Everything she has on looks grubby, and I think she is very poor. At first, I thought she was delivering a parcel, I could see her putting quite a large object on a doorstep, but now I can see that it is a basket with a baby inside. A very new baby that she's leaving. She's crying as she does it, but I think she just can't afford this baby.' Cassie scoffed, 'The same old problem the world over.'

'How sad. What happens next?' Sara prompted.

'I am being shown a series of snapshots of this child as he grows up. It's a boy and the family behind the doorway took him in. He is looked after by them with the basics of food and housing given to him, but he is their servant. I'm not being shown love or cuddles at all. He is always made aware that he owes them for taking him in. He is taunted by the other children in the village, and by the family as well sometimes. Everyone knows that his real mother abandoned him and they all tease him about it, saying that he wasn't wanted and was obviously of no good to her. He is full of anger for his real mother and his situation. I feel as if he is very bitter about his life in general.'

There was a pause as Cassie took in some more information that her Guide was showing her. 'I think that he eventually lashes out at the man of the family, while he's taunting him about being unwanted, and they throw him out. I'm not sure what happens next, I'm not really being shown anything else.'

'Maybe that's all we need to know,' Sara offered. 'Maybe that is the root of the anger, being taunted and teased about being not wanted in this past life. Never feeling any love, just being obligated to the family, and having to suffer their comments and behaviour. It's an awful situation to be in.'

'Horrible,' Cassie agreed.

'So, let's see if we can help the boy in this lifetime, release all that anger. Let's reframe what happened to him. Just go back to the beginning of the story and see the family taking in both the baby and his mother. They give them a couple of rooms to live in and plenty of food, and in return, the boy's mother works hard for the family. The family are loving and kind and the boy grows up with his mother and with a lot of love and cuddles. Let's see him being the centre of attention but in a loving way. Every member of the family, and his mother, find time to do things with him and he grows up happy, educated, and well looked after.'

Sara paused. 'Can you see that?'

'Yes, I can. He learns a new skill from each family member, and eventually, he marries a cousin, and the father gives them both some land and a hut, which they do up.' Cassie giggled slightly. 'I like doing this. I can see them standing tall and being confident and self-assured.'

'Good,' Sara said, smiling at the imagery in her mind. 'Okay, let's come back to your Guide and see if there is anything else that we need to do.'

'No, I don't think there is. She says that the release will be like a ripple, it will spread through all his lifetimes, through his life as Matteo, and eventually through his life as Joel.'

'Good. Well done, Cassie. It will be interesting to see what happens in this lifetime.' 'Is there anything else that we need to do to finish the session?' Sara added.

'No, I think that's it'.

'Okay, lovely. Let's just slowly come back into the present time and into this room by wriggling your fingers and your toes, and becoming aware of the cushions below you, and when you are ready, slowly open your eyes.'

Sara slowly opened her own eyes and did the same, wriggling her fingers and toes and having a stretch as she waited for Cassie to come back to the here and now.

Cassie slowly turned her head, looking at Sara and smiling broadly. 'That was so vivid. Matteo was so sad though. Why on earth couldn't he just talk to me?'

'I have no idea,' Sara replied. 'It is sad and, obviously,

because the lessons weren't learnt in that lifetime, some of them are repeating again through Joel.'

Cassie nodded as she pulled herself up to a sitting position. Sara handed her a glass of water and watched intently as she took a sip.

'I know this is hard for you and quite a shock to see that. I'm here for any support that you need,' she rubbed Cassie's shoulder gently in a comforting gesture.

'Thank you. I know you are, and I know I have lots of support around me. In a funny way, seeing that has made me feel more empowered and determined that Joel will not negatively affect me in this life. I'm sure he's not going to try and kill me, well, I certainly hope not, but he is messing with my life by having an affair and playing with my emotions. God knows what subsequent effects are going to play out. For all we know, Ava has told him to get rid of me, not by killing me this time, but by leaving me.'

Sara nodded gently. 'Yes, I get that. It doesn't have to necessarily play out the same way this time, but as you say, his actions are affecting you in a negative way. Now that you have seen that, and if you can get an understanding of the lessons that are playing out, the situation may well shift and start healing. The fact that we were able to reframe the situation is also going to help.'

'That's interesting,' Cassie answered. 'So, even without the reframing, by me seeing and understanding the situation, healing can start to occur, and the situation may morph and change from that lifetime?'

'Yes, absolutely. Maybe you can come out of it this time in a much more positive way?'

'I hope so,' Cassie said, deep in thought. Images from the session kept coming into her mind, and she felt foggy, as if she hadn't quite come out of trance yet.

'Let me make us a cup of tea and get some biscuits to bring us around,' Sara advised, getting up and making her way to the kitchen. 'I think you need to ground a bit more before you go.'

The Binding Spell

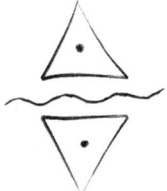

Sophia pottered around the conservatory, pumping up cushions, dusting over the few ornaments that decorated the windowsills, and picking off the odd dead leaf as she noticed them on her beloved plants. She found a couple of large white candles from her 'spare cupboard' and placed them on the coffee table, together with a box of matches and a box of incense that she had bought from the Angel Shop that day. Martha had suggested that she cleanse the conservatory before their session today and had advised her that one way was through incense. 'Just waft a lighted incense stick around, especially in the corners of the room, with the intention to clear any negative energy that has accumulated there,' she had told Sophia. 'It's a lovely way to clean the energy of a room and so important before a meditation session or a session like the one we'll be doing.'

Sophia carefully lit one of the incense sticks, tentatively sniffing at the smoke that slowly curled upwards, and was pleasantly surprised by its scent. 'Oh, that's lovely,' she said out loud to herself as she followed Martha's instructions, wafting the cleansing smoke into the corners of the room. When she had finished, she carefully stuck the remainder of the incense stick in the little shell holder that she had also bought and left it to continue to gently scent the room.

Finally, Sophia collected the few crystals that she had dotted about the house. She had always liked crystals and been fascinated by the different colours and shapes, so had bought a few over the years whenever they had caught her eye. Today she found a beautiful white quartz cluster, a smaller piece of rough pink quartz, and a very sparkly, pale blue celestite. She arranged the three crystals together around the candle and felt the excitement in her rise. Tonight, she and Martha were going to try and talk to Cassie from her past life. She had no idea if that was possible, all of this was so far outside of her comfort zone, but she was guided by her friend who had so much more experience than her. Whether it was possible or not, she thought, it would be interesting to try, and if they were successful, maybe they would be able to help Cassie now. If the Magus could give them some guidance as to how Cassie could change the outcome of her current life, then maybe Cassie and Joel could heal their differences. Sophia didn't want to interfere in her son's marriage, but she was furious with him for his behaviour, and could see no reason why she couldn't speak to her daughter-in-law about the matter whether it was in this lifetime or another!

Once the conservatory was set up to Sophia's satisfaction, she made her way into the kitchen to prepare some dinner for them both. She had decided on a traditional Portuguese soup – which was easy to make and she knew Martha loved. Sophia had bought some fresh bread rolls to go with it whilst she had been in town, together with a couple of custard tarts which she and Martha just adored from the little bakery on the high street.

Once she had the soup gently bubbling away, she quickly went to change and make herself look a little more presentable. She knew her friend wouldn't care less what she had on, but she wanted to make an occasion of it.

As Sophia made her way down the stairs in a fresh white blouse and comfortable stretchy jeans, she heard Martha calling her name from the back door. Her friend had not used the front door in the last thirty years, she thought, chuckling to herself as she went to greet her.

'So, what happens first?' Sophia asked Martha as she bent to light the candles on the coffee table. The flickering light caught the many reflective faces of the crystals and made them glisten and twinkle. Sophia turned off the main light and the room immediately felt cosy and atmospheric. She then shut the door to the house and turned on the storage heater on the far wall – just to warm the room slightly. She and Martha settled into cane chairs opposite each other, each with a comfy flowered cushion to lean on and a colourful woollen rug to pull over their knees if the temperature dropped too much.

'Well, I think we should open up first,' suggested Martha.

Sophia raised her eyebrows slightly 'Open up?' she asked questioningly.

'Sorry,' Martha smiled, 'it's just a term meaning to expand our energies, which helps to raise our vibration so that it is easier for us to connect to Spirit and to our guides. Hopefully, also easier to connect to the Red Magus,' she offered.

'The red Magus?' Sophia. 'Why red?'

'Well, she has vivid red hair, so it seemed a good title for her until we know her real name,' Martha said.

'Okay, Red Magus it is,' agreed Sophia. 'So, show me how to open up.'

Martha expertly and quickly took Sophia through the process of expanding her energy, connecting to a beautiful shaft of brilliant white light from the Universe above, and balancing the energies by connecting to a golden grounding energy from the centre of the earth. As the two mixed within their energy fields, she guided Sophia to connect to her breath, allowing her energy field to slowly expand with each out breath. Once they had expanded their energies, Martha then grounded them both within the room, sending golden streams of light down into the earth from each corner. After a full fifteen minutes, she instructed Sophia to slowly open her eyes and come back into the room. Eventually, they were both back to full awareness, looking at each other across the flickering light.

'I'm going to see if I can connect to the Red Magus now,' Martha said, closing her eyes again and focusing on her breath. Each breath seemed exaggerated but eventually, as Sophia watched, she could see Martha's breath subside to a more normal rate, and her eyelids began to flicker rapidly as she gently went into a deeper level of meditation. 'I can see her' Martha said, 'in the distance, as if she is at the end of a long tunnel. I'm asking my guides to bring her forward so that I can see her more clearly.' There was a long pause before Martha said, 'Thank you, I can see her clearer now.'

Martha began to describe the image of the Red Magus to Sophia, how she was dressed in a long, coarsely woven, blue dress, tied in the middle with a rope-like belt. There was a line of pouches hanging from it, in all different sizes and shapes, together with the dried skull of a bird or some other animal, which hung alongside. Martha wasn't quite sure what animal it came from but was not impressed with the macabre omen, although when the Magus explained that it was used in protection rituals, she felt a little more comfortable with its image. The Red Magus had a red chiffon-like scarf wrapped around her copper tresses, the tones of which clashed strangely, and on her cheeks and forehead were black and red symbols drawn on with a substance like wet ash, and the red dust from where she lived. Her eyes were large and dark brown, beautiful in fact, eyes that you could almost lose yourself in they had such depth. Her hands were dirty, smeared with red dust and the ash from her face. Martha could see that her fingernails were equally black. She looked dishevelled slightly and Martha got the impression that life was tough. There was no luxury for the Red Magus, but she managed to not only survive but to thrive in this harsh landscape where she lived. She was a beautiful woman, Martha concluded. She had strong features and an arresting stature and clearly felt confident and empowered in her world.

'Okay, what do we want to ask her?' Martha asked Sophia whilst opening her eyes.

'Oh, I'm not sure now,' Sophia panicked slightly. 'Let's just ask her straight: what does Cassie need to do now?' Sophia suggested.

Martha slowly closed her eyes. 'Okay,' she said. There was a long pause and Sophia realised she was almost holding her breath as she waited for Martha to speak. She took a deep breath and concentrated on breathing calmly and smoothly. It was so long before Martha spoke that Sophia began to wonder if she had dropped off.

'Okay,' Martha suddenly said, making Sophia jump slightly. 'The Red Magus is telling me that, because Cassie has made this connection to her across time and space, she is now able to send her information and energy through the energetic connection that they have created. A bit like forming a pipe between the two worlds so that they can each send things through to the other. In essence, they are the same soul energy, learning in different lifetimes, but at the same time. These lives are happening simultaneously so they can contact each other easily across the thin veil of energy that separates them. Because of this close connection, the Red Magus can help Cassie, or herself, if you like. She keeps referencing the symbols on her face, how powerful they are, and that they can help Cassie access different frequencies of energy which she may not have been able to do beforehand. I think these symbols are what she uses to amplify her energy. However, Cassie already knows and understands this at some level as they are both the same soul and therefore have access to the same information. Once Cassie becomes aware of this ability in this lifetime, there will be a remembrance and she will know what to do.'

Sophia's forehead crinkled slightly. She didn't understand what Martha meant by that or any of it, to be honest, but she quickly picked up the notepad and pen she'd left on the coffee table and made some notes so she could ask her later.

'The Red Magus was warning her about a woman who has red hair like hers. You know Cassie told us that the red hair in her sessions was vivid, whilst everything else was subdued, well it was because the Red Magus wanted her to get the connection. Obviously, we now know that Joel has been seeing someone with red hair so that was what it was about.' Martha opened her eyes to look briefly at her friend with concern and then closed them again.

Sophia felt a heaviness in her heart. She had suspected that Joel was having an affair, but this confirmation saddened her greatly. Somehow, she felt responsible in part. He was her son after all, and she realised that she was ashamed of him in that moment. She felt a lump rise in her throat and she took a sip of water to try and wash it away.

'The Red Magus is angry, not just at Joel, but that this betrayal is happening again. She seems to be referencing the fact that this is a thread that has been going on in her Soul Continuum for life after life, and she is furious that any of her future lives could be about the same lesson.'

Sophia realised she was holding her breath again. It took her a few minutes to catch up with what Martha was saying. It was like a different language, she thought. 'How can we help her change this? Can we help?' Sophia asked.

'I think we must work out what lesson the thread is related to, and then Cassie can understand it, review it, and perhaps let it go so it doesn't have to be repeated. It could be about betrayal and fidelity, but also about Cassie setting clear boundaries, not getting lost in a relationship, and her own self-esteem. What do you think?' Martha opened her eyes to look at Sophia.

Sophia's mouth opened and closed slightly as she tried to process all the information that she had just received. 'I'm not sure,' she offered weakly.

Martha closed her eyes again. 'Don't worry we'll work it out,' she said.

There was another pause as Martha continued to silently converse with the Red Magus. 'I think she's saying that she's done a binding spell for Cassie,' she said, with amazement in her voice. 'Apparently, she does them for others in her lifetime. Where there's another woman or someone that's interfering, she can stop them so that they don't affect the paths of the people involved.'

'How will she do that?' Sophia asked, slightly concerned for Joel.

'She's showing me a wax figure which she's moulding with her hands.' There was a pause as Martha was obviously watching and trying to decipher what the figure looked like. 'Oh,' she finally said and opened her eyes suddenly. She looked slightly shocked and Sophia was concerned.

'What is it?' she asked.

'Well, it looks like a woman with her hands and feet bound behind her back. It wasn't very nice but I'm guessing that the binding is not physical, it's energetic. If I understand correctly, she'll be binding the woman on an energetic level so that she cannot manipulate or affect Joel in any way. I'm assuming that this will bind his feelings for this woman at the same time as well.

'It's the woman he's having an affair with that will be bound.' She opened her eyes again, 'that's not a bad thing, is it?'

'No, not at all! I think that's the best solution, to be honest. If it means that Joel will lose interest, then that's great,' Sophia said. 'Just check that nothing will happen to Joel.'

Martha looked at her for a moment, shut her eyes and appeared to converse again with the Red Magus. Sophia felt a wave of anxiety rise through her as she waited for a reply. She knew Joel was in the wrong but she was his mother and didn't want any harm to come to him. She was ashamed of his actions but again her love for him overwhelmed the need for any punishment to be carried out. She knew in her heart that he would lose Cassie and Xander and that would surely be punishment enough.

Martha seemed to take forever before she opened her eyes and looked at her friend. 'No. I don't think so,' she said softly.

Sophia's brow crinkled slightly. 'Really? That was all she said after all that time?'

'Well, I was trying to talk her out of doing anything to Joel,' Martha whispered leaning forward towards her friend as if the Red Magus was in the room and would hear her and be offended. 'She wanted to disrupt his energy field somehow but I was trying to pursue her not to.'

'Oh, sorry Martha. You're a good friend and I should have known you would do that.' Sophia smiled weakly at her friend. 'So, do you think she agreed to leave him alone?'

'Yes, I think so. If the first binding spell on the woman works, then she won't need to do anything else, will she.'

'Let's hope not,' Sophia sighed. 'Anything else we can do to help?'

Martha closed her eyes again. Eventually, she said, 'I think the woman's name is Eve or Eva or something short like that. I was never good at hearing names, but it seems to be in that format. Has Joel mentioned anyone with a name like that?'

'No, he doesn't talk to me about his friends or work colleagues. We'll have to ask Cassie. Anything else?' Sophia asked.

'She's showing me where she lives in her lifetime. It's like the place is hewn into the rock. There are lots of narrow pathways between the rock faces and everything is very red. I don't know whether that is my imagination, but it seems like the rock itself is very red in colour. It's dusty and hot and there are all sorts of people milling around. They look like they are traders, all selling different goods. It's like some sort of film set. I wish you could see it.' Martha smiled with her eyes still shut, as if she was indeed enjoying watching a film in her mind's eye. 'I've never seen something like this before. I think the Red Magus is so powerful energetically that she's enhancing what I am seeing and understanding. I've never seen things so clearly in a session before. It's amazing!'

Sophia smiled at her friend and sat back in her chair, allowing Martha to enjoy the experience that was happening to her. 'She's showing me that she works in a temple and has a home there. Her ancestors were nomadic, walking across the desert between different settlements to sell their wares, but she has a static home now. It's hewn into the red rock, and she seems very proud that she owns it by herself, as a woman. I understand that she sells curse dolls and tablets. The tablets look as if they have spells written on them,' Martha tilted her head slightly whilst relaying what she was seeing to Sophia, as if she was listening as well.

'Can you hear her?' Sophia asked.

'I can't hear her voice but I seem to be collecting all this information she's giving me through all my senses. It's hard to explain, but it's a mixture of visual, sound and knowing and it comes together in a vivid three-dimensional depiction. Like I say, this isn't normal for me. The Red Magus is amplifying everything with her energy.'

Sophia smiled to herself, shaking her head slightly. She had no idea what her friend was experiencing, but she could tell from watching Martha that it was incredible, and her friend was totally awed. She waited patiently for a while until Martha eventually opened her eyes and looked at her smiling broadly. 'Wow!! That was extraordinary. The Red Magus is very powerful, which means Cassie is as well if only she was able to tap into it!' Martha exclaimed. 'If Cassie knew what she was capable of then this would be a very different story. But then I suppose that's the point, isn't it?'

'What is?' Sophia asked, feeling slightly out of her depth.

'Well, if Cassie had learnt in this lifetime how truly powerful she was, then she wouldn't lack self-confidence and she wouldn't allow anyone to take advantage of her. That's her lesson for this lifetime, to learn how empowered she truly is. She had a rough start in foster homes and since Xander was born she hasn't been herself, and that's understandable. Having a child is hard work, but there's something else as well. It's as if all her self-confidence has just ebbed away. We must try and get her to see that she's more powerful than she would ever imagine.' Martha finally paused and looked at her friend. 'Sorry, I'm getting a bit carried away, but it was so amazing.'

Sophia chuckled slightly, 'Don't worry at all. I can see how pumped you are about the whole experience, and rightly so. You've just had a conversation with a woman who lives in a different dimension! It is amazing!' and she shook her head slightly at her friend.

The excitement that they both felt continued for the rest of the evening and the two friends chatted incessantly as they tucked into Sophia's delicious supper.

'Talking across aeons of time and space has made me hungry!' Martha exclaimed and they both laughed at the absurdity of it all. After eating and discussing in depth their session with the Red Magus, the two friends eventually hugged good night, and Martha made her way through the back door, and the small gap in their mutual fence which she always used. When Sophia and Patrick had first moved in, only a couple of years after Martha and Roger, all those years ago, they had spoken about blocking up the gap. However, the ensuing friendship meant that it never happened, and the gap had been Martha's choice of access ever since.

Martha realised that she was shocked by the evening's events and felt as if she was still in a trance as she made her way slowly up to her bedroom. She didn't feel traumatised by the events, but she did feel fascinated and excited by them. Roger was sleeping soundly. She could hear his regular breathing and could make out his shape as he lay on his side in the darkness. Martha tiptoed in the dark to the ensuite to change into her pyjamas and carry out her usual ablutions, and then gently and quietly climbed into the space beside him. She leant up on her elbow and held herself very still for a minute, listening intently as to whether she had disturbed him, but there was no disruption to his breath, and she settled down to sleep...

The light appeared to be made up of many individual threads, which spread out from a central point. The effect was of a slightly uneven pillar of light, as if fanned out at the bottom. The craggy red rocks were highlighted in places by the light and its erratic reflections, and the colours were a palette of pinks and reds, and then greys and blacks around the periphery of the scene where the light couldn't reach. The Red Magus stood naked in the main pool of light, her long, wet, copper tresses spread in a fan across the smooth skin of her back, her arms and hands reaching up as if to embrace the beams of light. Martha could see that there was a stream of water gently rippling over the rocks at her feet, and she realised that the Red Magus had been washing herself in advance of this meeting. The light began to pulse slightly as if it was speaking in some unheard language, and its intensity seemed to embrace the body of the Red Magus so that she became less and less defined, and appeared to be vanishing within the light until there was only an impression of where she stood. Martha watched the scene for a while sensing that there was information being exchanged in some way through this beautiful light streaming through the opening in the roof of the cave, and the Red Magus. The light, the colours, and the pulsing were hypnotic, and Martha was sure that it had sent her off into a deeper trance for a while. She had no sense of time, or how long the vision had lasted, but suddenly the light flashed and exploded into a fireball of reds and pinks, out of which a large black crow emerged, spreading its wings, and cruising slowly in an arc out of the portal in the ceiling of the cave. As it did so, it cawed loudly, and Martha sat bolt upright in her bed, her eyes wide open and her breath erratic and laboured. A strange sound escaped her lips, the sound of which woke both Martha and Roger fully.

'What on earth!' Roger exclaimed. 'What's the matter, what's going on? Is it one of the girls?' He had grabbed Martha by the arm as he struggled to escape sleep and be fully present and aware.

'I'm sorry,' Martha managed to gasp. 'It's okay, Roger, I'm okay and so are the girls. Just a strange dream,' and she patted his hand which still held her firmly by the arm.

'Are you sure?' Roger softened, as he turned to sit fully upright and put his arms around his wife. 'What were you dreaming of?'

'I'm not sure,' Martha lied. 'But I'm fine, honestly. Something just made me jump.' She pulled herself out of his arms slightly to look him in the eyes and reassure him. 'I'm fine. Go back to sleep.'. She patted his hand again.

Roger scoffed a little, 'After that? I don't think so. You scared me half to death!' He swung his legs over his side of the bed and pushed himself up to make his way slowly, and a little groggily to the ensuite. 'I think I'll have a shower,' and the door shut firmly behind him.

Martha lay on her back with her eyes wide open, breathing deeply. The dream had been so vivid and had shocked her. It felt more like something the Red Magus was showing her rather than a dream, and Martha wondered whether she hadn't shown her everything she had wanted to from the night before. Martha went through the scenes again in her head. Was she talking to someone and, if so, who? Why was she talking through a cave opening? Why was there a crow? Martha glanced at her digital clock at the side of the bed and saw that it was almost 7 a.m. She swung her legs out of bed and made her way downstairs for some coffee. She would check in on Sophia later and see what she thought.

'So, what do you think it was about?' Martha asked a few hours later. She was leaning on Sophia's kitchen island, a large mug of coffee in her hand. It was just past eleven and with all the excitement of the last few hours, Martha had decided that she could have one more coffee. Much more and she wouldn't sleep that night.

'I'm not sure it was a dream, more like some further information being given to you,' Sophia agreed. 'But what she was doing and why, I don't know. The washing is probably a purification thing, as if preparing herself for a ritual. But who she was talking to is unclear. The way you describe the pulsing light brings God to mind.'

Martha raised her eyebrows at her friend.

'Well, Spirit then, if that's what you would prefer to call it,' Sophia added, seeing her reaction.

'Well, I can take Spirit,' Martha said. 'Maybe that was the way she could show me that she speaks to Spirit like I do?'

'A depiction of Spirit?' Sophia suggested.

'Exactly!' Martha replied.

'That certainly makes sense. Maybe for her, it was a ritual, and her way of preparing and speaking to Spirit.'

'I'm not sure about the crow though. It was as if she turned into the crow. Do you think she can shapeshift?' Martha asked.

'Gosh, well that does make this whole thing feel a bit like a science fiction film,' Sophia answered.

'Yes, you're right,' Martha chuckled. 'Perhaps it's more symbolic. What does a crow mean spiritually?'

Sophia shrugged her shoulders, paused for a moment, and then suggested, 'Let's Google it.'

'Crows are usually seen as positive, depicting transformation, destiny, intelligence, fearlessness, mystery, adaptability and a higher perspective,' Martha said, reading from her phone. 'Well, all of those meanings fit, don't they?' she said looking up at Sophia.

'Yes, absolutely. Everything that's been playing out recently.'

'They also represent death and are considered messengers from the other side! Wow! No wonder she was showing me a crow. How clever she is!' Martha exclaimed.

The Queue

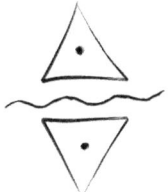

Cassie and Sara sat side by side in Sara's beautiful treatment room, gazing at the array of crystals as they chatted. They had enjoyed a lovely refreshing cup of tea together as they prepared for their next past life regression session. 'I really love that green one,' Cassie said, pointing to a small blue-green specimen. 'What is it?'

'This one?' Sara had risen and was now pointing to a little natural crystal sitting on the third shelf of her crystal display.

'Yes, it's lovely. It looks waxy somehow.'

'It's blue green calcite. The calcites are lovely stones, they come in all sorts of colours, but blue green calcite is a very powerful crystal. It will soothe and relax the emotions and is also very protective for your energy field. Just what you need.' Sara smiled, picked up the crystal and handed it to Cassie. 'Why don't you have it with you for the session? If it's jumping out at you then you obviously need its vibration.'

'Thanks, yes, I will,' said Cassie smiling at Sara, carefully examining the contours of the crystal at different angles as she turned it in her hand.

Nowadays, Cassie needed little help to go into trance and was easily in a deep state of relaxation almost before the session started. She could feel herself slipping into this state as she settled down on the cushions in Sara's treatment room, preparing herself for the hour or so ahead. As she closed her eyes, she was already seeing a line of figures standing behind her and she began to explain what she was seeing immediately.

Sara was slightly taken aback by the speed of the information that was coming to Cassie, but not surprised either. She had known almost immediately what a powerful spiritual force her friend was or could become if she just allowed herself to flow with it, which Cassie had done. She smiled to herself now with both a little envy and a great deal of pride for the way Cassie was developing and dealing with this influx of visions and strange information.

'I can see this line of figures going on and on behind me as if we're queuing for something,' Cassie began, chuckling slightly at the idea of queuing in spirit.

'Who are they?' Sara asked leaning forward, her elbow on her knee and her hand cupping her face as she listened intently. She always found their sessions fascinating. It was like reading an amazing novel and not being able to wait for the next chapter.

There was a pause as Sara watched Cassie breathe slowly in and out before saying, 'They have shown themselves to me before. They are my ancestors, I think. There is a long line of mostly women behind me, but they are all masters of their own time.'

'In what way?' Sara probed, her brows knitted tightly as she tried to understand.

'Well, they each became highly skilled in their own lives.' Cassie paused. 'I don't think they are my ancestors as such, but each represents one of my past lives, and therefore is an aspect of my soul energy. Each character represents a time when I had mastered an aspect of energy. How cool is that?!' Cassie suddenly exclaimed, chuckling but not opening her eyes.

'Very cool indeed. How interesting that you can see them all together in a line across time and space. Think about all the innate wisdom and knowledge that you have available in your soul to tap into,' Sara offered.

'I hadn't thought about it like that but you're right. I already know what they know, I just need to access it.' Cassie suddenly went very quiet, seemingly emotional and overwhelmed by the fact that she had so much knowledge available to her and that she was able to see and understand this. 'My own internal library,' she finally offered, trying to smile through her emotion as she said it.

'Yes, exactly. We must all have streams of information and knowledge that we can tap into then. That's such an empowering concept, isn't it? Can you tune into any of the figures or past lives that they represent?'

Sara waited with bated breath as Cassie lay there, seemingly sleeping peacefully, she was so still but was, in fact, gaining further information and insights from her guides. She smiled and shook her head in awe at how interesting this therapy was for her.

Eventually, Cassie began to speak again. 'The first figure that jumps out is a man. I get that he's in his forties but very small in stature and he only has a loin cloth on, a headdress, and armbands made of twine with stones and twigs interwoven. The headdress is the same and they represent his close connection with nature and Gaia. It feels as if he lives in a jungle, its thick dense tropical-looking foliage. He has very dark hair and eyes, and his skin is covered in mud.' She paused then exclaimed, 'He's a witch doctor!'

There was another pause as Cassie seemed to be listening or sensing the information about this man. 'Yes, he's a witch doctor for his tribe. He helps with physical problems and with keeping the dark spirits at bay. I feel as if they believe that everything – including the rocks, trees, and streams – has spirit and these spirits can become cross or upset, which can affect them physically, mentally, or spiritually. He's the main figure in the tribe. He feels very proud and strong. Very solid in his role.'

Before Sara could ask any questions, Cassie continued. 'The next figure stepping forward is an older woman. She's got a long, rough dress and apron on, and she collects herbs. I think she has red hair! Another red-haired woman,' Cassie scoffed slightly. 'I think she's Scottish, living in a hut in rolling countryside. It feels wet and cold. It's a hard life but she loves the solitude.' Cassie involuntarily shivered slightly. 'But really cold,' she added again. 'She collects herbs and administers them for the local farmers and their animals. She's a healer, if you like.'

'So, both figures are healers and caregivers in their own way?' Sara asked.

'Yes, that's right,' Cassie said. 'That's interesting, isn't it? Maybe that's what the thread is about? But I'm not a healer.'

'Well, you may be,' Sara said, 'you just haven't tried yet.'

'Maybe,' Cassie said hesitantly.

'Can you sense any of the other characters?' Sara asked.

'Yes, there's a young girl. She's about fifteen I think, with a dress to her knees and a dirty apron over the top. A bit like the herb lady but she's in a town or city. I don't know where, but it doesn't feel like England. There's a huge Cathedral with large figures carved on the outside, and animals being sold in the market square. There's straw on the floor and…' Cassie paused as she seemed to look around the scene. 'There are lights all around the square, marking it out, like metal cages with a fire inside, on top of a post, if that makes sense. There also appears to be gallows.' Her voice softened as she realised this.

There was a long pause and then Cassie said, 'I think she's showing me that she was hung because she was different. She could see the souls of people passing over. In a time when religion was important and people were God-fearing, she believed that God was loving and all-embracing. She was killed because of her abilities and her beliefs.'

The room felt intensely still and quiet. 'How sad,' Sara commented. 'How interesting that she is also in your thread. Maybe this isn't just about healers, but about psychic abilities, if you wish?'

'Yes, definitely. Being able to see and manipulate energy seems to be a theme. It's not the only one but it's one of them. So, that means I must have some ability to do that as well, doesn't it?'

'It would appear so,' Sara said. 'But you are already doing that by connecting to the Magus. She is giving you information across time and space, which is to your advantage, and can change the course of both of your lives.'

'Yes, I suppose I am.'

'And you can get this information from a session, which is amazing. That's a real ability.'

'I suppose so. I hadn't thought about it like that, it's just the norm for me now.'

'I don't think you realise how this is not normal for most of my sessions,' Sara advised her friend. 'Lots of my clients really struggle to see or feel as you do, and they often don't get the information from their guides as you can. Visuals are also quite unusual and it's not common to see things like a film projected on a screen. You are already showing that you have amazing psychic abilities.'

'I didn't realise that,' Cassie said slowly and softly, as the realisation sunk in that she was seeing and knowing information from different dimensions and in ways that were not considered the norm. 'Wow!' she eventually whispered. 'I was so intent on trying to understand why I was seeing this stuff, that I didn't think about how good it was to be able to see at all!'

'Exactly!' Sara said. 'You already have amazing gifts and powers. Why don't you ask them if one of them would like to give you a message that can help you in this current lifetime?'

'Okay, I will,' Cassie said and then fell silent.

Sara waited patiently in the stillness until Cassie spoke again.

'The Magus stepped forward as I asked that question. She is also in the queue or the thread if you like. She is an aspect of myself which feels so strong and feisty. She does not want us to keep having to live through the same lesson over and over again. In so many lifetimes we mastered energy and used it for our own highest will and good. I mean for the use of the whole human race, not just aspects of us. However, in other lives, we were persecuted for understanding and knowing about energy as it frightened people, so it was a real paradox. However, she is saying that in my current lifetime, these abilities are now much more widely accepted and that if we are totally able to step into our own power, and really show the world what we can do, then the lessons around being intimidated, hounded, and even killed for who we are, will be learnt. We won't have to suffer the same elements in our future lives but can concentrate on other lessons like expanding our knowledge of energy and building on our abilities.'

Cassie paused and Sara breathed slightly deeper as she took in the power of the moment. Every one of us, she thought, must have these threads throughout our Soul energy that just keep repeating themselves until we can really understand them, truly step past them, and learn how amazing and powerful we are. It was a huge insight into why she found this work so amazing, and she felt inspired and empowered to do more spiritually.

Her eyes went back to Cassie, who lay statue still, breathing slowly and deeply, and she waited to see whether she wanted to say anything further.

'The Magus is talking about Joel and the fact that he has betrayed me,' her voice caught slightly in her throat. Sara immediately felt a wave of compassion wash over her. She knew how much the affair was hurting Cassie.

Cassie cocked her head slightly to one side, and her voice rose a little as she said, 'The Magus is offering to hurt him again! Well, I suppose I'm offering to hurt him!'

'How?' Sara asked as she tried to get her mind around this. 'What can she or you do?'

'Well, something about sending streams of energy. I've seen them before from her to me and to Joel, but Joel's are darker. If she makes it very dark and negative then it will affect his energy field in this lifetime and he would become unwell, even die.' Cassie felt shocked by the words that had just come out of her mouth, and her hands went instinctively to her heart. She was almost in tears as she said, 'Oh my God! I can't kill him!'

'Breathe slowly, Cassie,' Sara immediately moved seamlessly back into a professional mode as she helped Cassie to calm her breathing and her emotions. 'The Magus isn't saying you must do that, just that you can. Of course, you don't want to murder him or even harm him, but it's interesting that it's an option.'

'I don't know,' Cassie said, her voice a little harder as she pondered this notion, 'maybe making him regret what he's done would be a good thing. Maybe that will teach him a lesson that his soul needs to learn. His so-called girlfriend too.' Cassie suddenly turned her head and opened her eyes so that she was looking directly at Sara, 'Is that awful?' she asked.

'No, I don't think it's awful, just human. There are obviously lessons that both Joel and his girlfriend need to learn – infidelity, betrayal, anger, and manipulation for a start. It might be interesting to see how this energy stream works?'

Cassie looked at her friend again, smiling slightly, but no words needed to be spoken.

The Cave

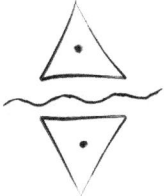

Hinat struggled to get out of bed. Her mind was racing but her body, and especially her swollen stomach, just couldn't follow as quickly. Her ankles had also swelled up these last few days and Hinat knew that the baby would be arriving very shortly. She attempted to roll over on her side several times, before managing to get some momentum and sitting up in one swift movement on the edge of the bed. She rubbed her stomach in reassurance, smiling down at her daughter with love, and then pushed herself to a standing position. Her heart was racing with excitement as she slowly made her way to the kitchen, her hair tousled from sleep and her feet still bare.

Hinat had dreamed of her father so clearly, that it had almost been as if he was standing in the room with her. He was chastising her for not being observant, for not seeing what was in front of her nose. Hinat had listened to him, excited to see him but also confused as to what he was talking about. What was she missing?

Her father had continued gesticulating and she had followed him as he had made his way into the kitchen. It was a long, narrow, and uneven room carved out of the rock itself, so the surface of the walls was rough and uneven and the room itself was asymmetrical, running to a longer point on one side. Her father and brothers had built shelves in a straight line across the rear wall many years before, so that the unevenness of the room was not immediately evident, and Hinat had never thought more about it. Now he was telling her to take down the shelves, but she didn't understand why. They had been there forever, and the extra storage was useful to her. Besides, Hagru would go mad if there was less storage space and nowhere to put anything, she reasoned. Hinat stood dumbfounded as she continued to watch her father instruct her how to remove the shelves. His image got brighter and brighter as if the intensity of his message was being heightened and, eventually, simply because she didn't know what else to do, she agreed, and he faded almost immediately.

Hinat woke with the image of her father and his instructions clear in her mind and now she stood in the kitchen, in her nightdress, staring at the shelves. Without thinking, she started clearing the bowls and kitchen utensils that lined the shelves in neat rows. The shelves were full of items and it was impossible to see behind them clearly without moving everything. As she did so, she wiped the shelves clean. These days she was very conscious of the cleanliness of the house and everything she did. It was the imminent arrival of the baby that was making her clean, she was sure. It had certainly amused Hagru who had wryly commented that she wasn't used to Hinat cleaning or tidying at all, much to Hinat's irritation, although she knew that it was indeed true. It had never been her job or something that she was even aware of until now.

Hinat stopped to make herself a hot tea, which she gently sipped whilst sitting on a stool, still in her night clothes, staring at the bare shelves. She could now see the red rock wall behind them and realised that there appeared to be a gap in the left-hand corner of the room. It was slight, and it was only because the light didn't appear to penetrate in the same way, that Hinat realised that there may well be a passageway. These homes, hewn into the rock, often contained nooks, crannies and passage-ways which led deeper into the rock itself. Hinat was shocked though. She had never noticed this before, and nobody in her family had ever mentioned it. It was only because of the dream that she was even aware of the possibility of it. She finished her tea, enjoying the short but well-earned rest, and quickly dressed. Hinat was just leaving as Hagru arrived, and she instructed the shocked maid not to replace anything on the shelves. Hinat allowed her gaze to sweep across the kitchen which was so full of utensils that it was almost impossible to walk across the room.

'Just clean some other room for now,' Hinat instructed her. 'Please,' she added as she saw her maid's expression. 'It's important. My brothers are going to come and take down the shelves, so don't put anything on them,' she instructed again for emphasis as she swiftly exited the house, avoiding the stern and bemused gaze of Hagru.

Her brothers were equally bemused as to Hinat's request to come to the house immediately and to dismantle the old wooden shelves in the kitchen, which had been there for years. 'Why?' her eldest brother Sami asked, shrugging his shoulders, and raising his hands. 'Why Hinat? We all have jobs to do and really don't need to be involved in this whim,' he added sternly.

Hinat sighed. 'Father told me,' she said quietly and quickly explained the dream to him. 'I think it's important.' Of course, he couldn't refuse to help, knowing that Hinat had such a strong connection to both their father and Spirit, but was surprised that she had not known this earlier. 'Maybe I wasn't meant to know before now? Maybe now is the correct time. Everything happens at the correct time,' she added wisely. Her brother nodded and, collecting up his tools, followed her to the house.

Within a couple of hours, the wooden shelves were dismantled, and the wood neatly stacked on the floor, along one wall of the kitchen. Hinat and Sami stood carefully peering into the gap in the corner and could see that there was an opening, but it was dark and narrow so the extent of it wasn't clear at all. It could lead to nowhere, Hinat thought to herself, doubts beginning to creep into her mind. Hinat wasn't sure she could fit through the small entrance in her condition, and she certainly didn't want to get stuck halfway through. Of course, Sami thought this was hilarious, much to Hinat's irritation. She was often feeling irritated these days for a variety of reasons, but she knew that it would pass once the baby arrived. 'You'll have to go,' she said, finding it difficult not to sound aggrieved.

'Why don't you go when you've had the baby?' Sami suggested. 'I know you want to explore and see what Father wanted you to find, so why not wait until you can fit and are more agile?' his smile and accompanying giggle irritated her further.

'No. I think I need to find this now, so you'll have to go yourself. I'll get you a candle,' she said, digging in a box near the door of the kitchen. 'If we wrap the bottom of the candle with cloth, it won't drip and burn you. What do you think?' and she held the wrapped candle up to show him.

'What if there's a draught and it blows out?' he asked, looking concerned. 'If I get lost in some passageways I could get lost forever.'

'True. I think there should be two or more of you, and you should use twine to find your way. Tie it up here somewhere, and then let it unravel as you go. If you lose the light, you can follow it back.'

'Good idea. I'll go and see Josef on the way home and see if he'll help. It could lead somewhere amazing or nowhere at all. Some new rooms could be nice though,' he added.

'Thanks, Sami, I appreciate you coming over to help.' Hinat smiled at her brother, and then just as quickly her smile turned to a grimace and she bent over slightly, gasping as she did.

'Are you okay?' Sami asked with concern. 'Is the baby coming?' His voice rose slightly as he enquired of his younger sister.

Hinat nodded without speaking and Sami sprang into action. He had two small boys of his own and knew exactly what to do. 'I'll let Zina know. And inform the doula on the way,' he added. 'Will you be okay until we all get back?'

Hinat straightened, breathing a little more easily as she did. 'I'll be fine,' she smiled. 'Go and fetch everyone and I'll be here when you return.' She pushed his shoulder gently as she made her way back to her bedroom. The baby was coming at last and she was so excited.

The labour was hard work, just as labour is supposed to be, as the doula advised her often, and Hinat chanted her way through it. The doula had explained that there was a link between the tissues of the throat and uterus, and chanting would aid the arrival of the baby. Hinat had readily tried it, and although it had not stopped the pain, the delivery had been relatively swift for a first child. Hinat was exhausted and her throat hurt with all the chanting she had done, but she was equally elated when, finally, her baby daughter, Celeste, was born. As she held this special soul in her arms, her tears fell with gratitude. She silently thanked her father for his help from the other side, whilst verbalising her thanks for the amazing doula and her sister-in-law who had been present with her the whole time. They had both been supportive and kind, and Hinat's heart swelled with the gratitude she had for them, and for the way they had held space for her and allowed her to naturally give birth.

Her family were surprised by the unusual name, which was more Mediterranean in origin, but Hinat was adamant. She had initially heard the name from some Greek traders who had made their way to Raqmu to sell their wares. Hinat had immediately been taken with it and when she explained to her family the connection to the celestite crystals which she used in the temple and their meaning of inner peace and elevating the spirit, they could understand the reasoning.

The whole family quickly became accustomed to this new addition and her unusual name, and the next few months were a blur of exhaustion and elation in equal measure as Hinat became used to being a mum. Celeste thrived with the love and attention bestowed on her and truly lived up to her name of being heaven-sent. She was a quiet baby, seemingly content from the moment she arrived. If she was fed well, then she would easily sleep, and Hinat was able to catch up on her own sleep or do a few chores.

Hinat recovered from the birth of her daughter quickly, staying at home for six weeks to allow her baby to get into a good routine, and establishing her breastfeeding, which was the tradition. On a couple of occasions, the baby had seemed to want to feed for an inordinate amount of time, but the doula had explained that she was naturally increasing her milk supply, and Hinat was able to relax and enjoy the time they had together. The doula and her sister-in-law, Zina, were always on hand during this initial time, to answer her questions and give her support when needed. However, they both seemed to know when to give her time alone as well, which Hinat appreciated. Omar had also visited on several occasions, seemingly smitten with his new daughter. Hinat knew that they would be friends and that he would always support them.

Hinat was sitting in bed one evening, feeding Celeste, when her mind wandered to the cave entrance for the first time since her brother had discovered it. She knew that she had to investigate further; the pull to discover more had been growing since the birth nearly seven weeks ago and was now undeniable. Once Celeste was full and had drifted off to sleep, Hinat wrapped her swaddling close around her and lay her in her crib. She knew that she had at least two hours, maybe a little more. Hinat quietly dressed, pulling her usual long dress up through her legs and tucking it into her belt. Nobody was going to see her, she reasoned, and she wanted to have the freedom to move her legs easily. She contemplated taking her dress off altogether, but decided it might be chilly, and continued fastening her skirt to her belt as securely as she could. Hinat tied her long tresses back in a ponytail, and then wrapped her head with a scarf, fastening it tightly on one side of her head. She didn't want to get any spiders or creepy crawlies stuck in her hair, and she shivered involuntarily at the thought. Once ready, she quietly backed out of the bedroom so as not to disturb Celeste and pulled the door ajar behind her. She made her way into the kitchen and quickly tied a ball of twine to a hook in the wall. She had made herself a similar makeshift candle to the one she had given her brother and, listening once more for any sound from the baby, and hearing nothing, she made her way through the slim entrance of the passageway.

The light from behind her illuminated the space for some time and then the candlelight began to take over. The passageway wasn't straight but had been formed by the boundary between what appeared to be two different rock surfaces. The boundary, which had opened enough to create this passageway, was curved, and Hinat had to lean to one side to slip through. It was barely the width of a person and, because of the uneven floor and walls, it was uncomfortable to manoeuvre through. It wasn't helped by the fact that she could feel that the ground sloped downwards, making her feel as if she was going to fall every step she took, but she kept going, desperate to see where it led. Hinat had a feeling that it would be somewhere quite special.

Eventually, the sloping rock gave way to a new piece of rock which appeared to block her path completely, and initially, Hinat thought this was the end of the passageway. However, moving the candle around so she could more clearly see the whole rock face in the small circle of light, she could see that there appeared to be a smaller tunnel below her waist height. Hinat knelt, shining the candle into the gap, and felt her excitement rapidly deflate. This frightened her. She didn't know where this tunnel went and once in it, she wouldn't be able to turn around. What if she got stuck and nobody found her? What if Celeste woke up and she wasn't there? The panic began to rise in her, and she had to take several breaths to calm herself down. Eventually, she felt better and, opening her eyes, noticed with surprise a small bee hovering in the candlelight. 'Where have you come from?' she asked out loud. Instantly she knew that this was a good omen and the bee had come to guide her. Tracing the bee's path with the light, she watched as it flew straight into the small tunnel. Placing her head in the entrance to try and follow it as long as possible, she noticed a slight breeze on her face and knew that this must lead to the outside somehow. Summoning all her courage, Hinat half crouched and half crawled into the space. She had to concentrate on her breath to keep her calm, and on her position so as not to hit her head on the rocks above as she clumsily moved forward, but suddenly the space opened, and she could make out a large cavern. Hinat gasped and laughed with delight all at once as she almost tumbled out of the confined space into the clearing. Her father had been right that there was a cave here, and now she had found it. She could no longer see the bee but carefully made her way down the slope of the floor directly in front of her until she found even ground. Looking down, she could see that she was standing on a large slab of smooth rock. Hinat knelt so that the candlelight in her hand illuminated the stone and could see that it was completely flat and unmarked, and had been placed there, rather than fallen randomly. She stepped to one side to try and make out what was around it, and realised that it had been placed over an underground stream, forming a tiny bridge. The stream was really nothing more than a gentle trickle, but it appeared to pool directly in front of the stone, making the wet rock beneath it a deep and almost blood-red colour. In the candlelight, the pool looked black, and Hinat thought it would be a great place to scry. As she gently waved the candle around, forming circles of light which then quickly faded, she could see that there were other stones placed in what appeared to be a circle, and these were marked with symbols and images. Hinat couldn't make out much in the dark and knew that she would have to bring a bunch of candles with her next time.

She looked around in the darkness and realised that the air wasn't as stale and thick as in the passageway, and she could smell fresh air. With all her excitement, she had forgotten the breeze in the tunnel and now turned in a circle, trying to find the input of air. She couldn't quite work out where it was coming from but realised that there must be another opening, other than the passageway she had entered by. She vowed to come back during the day when the cave might be naturally illuminated, but for now, she crouched down on the flat stone and allowed her free hand to trail gently in the pool of water.

The underground water system that served Raqmu was

sacred and greatly revered. Water was their lifeline in these sometimes harsh and hot conditions, and the nomads of the desert knew every underground watercourse and stream. It had been essential to them to know where they could locate water at any time during their travels, and this knowledge had often been used as a bargaining tool with other tribes. Sitting on the rock in the dark, Hinat thought hard as to which watercourse this little trickle may be attributed to. The water beneath her hand must have broken off from one of them, she thought. Presumably, there would be too many, and they would be too small, to keep a record of each one. How amazing to have this space with water beneath my home, she mused. Water was sacred and governed by water nymphs that many of her tribe worshipped. They would leave gifts and chant regularly at the many boreholes so that the waters never dried up and left them. On occasion, a borehole would dry up. This was usually because the underground stream had shifted slightly, and meant that a new borehole would have to be dug. This was hard and laborious work but her tribe knew the importance of their water knowledge and happily kept it fully updated and accurate.

Hinat knew that the water that flowed through this cave, and under Raqmu itself, had knowledge from Spirit and that it acted as a conduit between the different worlds and dimensions. It came direct from Source, and just like the crystals, could give her information and answers to her many questions. Many of her tribe could converse with the waters to gain this knowledge, usually through scrying – which they learnt from an early age. Others could cause the water to move in strange forms, almost like water tendrils coming out of the main water body, as their energy and the energy of the water combined, and the information sought was transferred directly into them as images and thoughts. It was amazing to watch and Hinat had seen it on many occasions, but she much preferred to scry, allowing the images to form within and on the water being used. Sometimes, by placing a finger or hand in the water, the images would intensify as if a stronger circuit had been created. She wondered whether water had come to her in this way so that she could learn more of its knowledge and wisdom and use it somehow with her curse dolls and tablets. How would that work, she wondered, as she made her way back up the slope to her kitchen above.

The next time Hinat entered the cave it was daylight, and as soon as she exited the short passageway that caused her to bend over double, she could see natural light flooding the cave. As she stepped out into the opening, her eyes became wide with wonder. She could see that there were stones in a geometric shape on the ground, all of which had symbols or images carved into them. In the centre was the large flat stone she had sat on previously, and below it the trickle and pool of never-ending water. The water must have been running along the same course for some time, she thought, as there was almost a channel in the earth, with the dark, wet, red colouring in the centre and lesser shades of orange and pink towards the edges, creating a beautiful striped effect. The pool, which had previously seemed black, appeared almost blood red in the daylight, and Hinat immediately knelt on the flat stone peering intently into the clear water. As she did so, she realised that the light was coming from a porthole directly above the central stone, and flinging her head back, she took in the column of sunlight flooding down into the cave. The porthole was small and circular, but the light spread further into a larger circle as it hit the central stone, like a spotlight from the world above. Around the edge of the porthole were irises that were growing on the earth above, their outer foliage drooping over where the earth gave way slightly, causing a fringe of flowers to form. That must be great camouflage from above, Hinat thought, nobody would see the porthole unless they were unfortunate enough to step into it. Scanning the cave from the central stone, Hinat could see that there were several irises growing around the central stone, as if marking out the circumference of light from above. She stooped over one, gently sniffing the familiar scent. She would use these to make her tinctures for the temple, she thought.

Hinat carefully made her way around the circle of marked stones to inspect the symbols, seeing several eye idols which were common in Raqmu. There were also suns in worship to their Sun God, and rippling lines obviously in homage to the sacred water and their Water God. There were hands, birds, plants, and crystals, and the crowstep decoration from the tombs, which signified access for her tribe and their dead to the Divine and the upper world above. There was also a symbol of two triangles with a wavy line between them, which she knew represented how water carried information from Spirit to the living below. All the symbols were common to her and her tribe and Hinat reasoned that a tribe member had probably set up this space, but there were also extra symbols and images which Hinat did not instantly recognise. She rubbed her hands over the strange pictures, brushing all the loose earth to one side to see more clearly what was below. For there to be symbols and images that she didn't recognise, then they had either fallen out of favour or someone who didn't belong to her tribe had carved them. Maybe what she could see was created by many visitors, over time, each adding their own decoration and homage to what was important to them. Hinat didn't know which version was correct but thought that she should also add something to represent her time in the cave. She would think about what was most appropriate, but instantly a bee came to her mind. They were so influential to her work and carried as much information as water did between the worlds. A bee had also helped her find the cave, so seemed very apt. Maybe she would add a bee or a symbol which could represent a bee, to some of the depictions and images already present. She smiled to herself. That would be her small but meaningful contribution to this sacred space of worship and knowledge. She felt truly blessed to be part of this space and to have this connection to those who had gone before her, and those that would come after her. Hinat could almost see a long line of participants stretching out behind her and in front of her. A long queue of souls of which she was one, connected and anchored by this one physical location. Maybe her father would give her some more information in another dream, as to what to contribute.

Hinat had brought some cleaning items with her this time and began to sweep the stones and create a clear space for her to come and carry out her worship and ceremonies – which she intended to do on a regular basis. On the rock face to the rear of the cave, she placed many candles on the rough little outcrops so that, once lit, they would create a shimmering wall of light. She didn't know whether she would come here at night, but if she did then she was prepared. As she carefully placed the candles, she discovered a couple of small stone carvings or betyls which had been placed in mini caves in the wall. These were obviously manmade, and Hinat cleared away the rubble and debris which had initially obscured them. She placed a candle in the middle of each, and reaching into her pocket, she added crystals and polished stones which she had brought with her – which would increase the shimmer when the candles were lit.

Hinat loved the shaft of sunlight that seemed almost solid as it flooded the cave and she sat on the flat stone, in the full force of the ray, with her hand trailing in the trickle of water below her. She prayed to Spirit and Dushara, the Sun God, for continual warmth, light and life. She thanked them both for blessing her with this space and called on Dushara to continue to flood the room with sunlight, and her life with joy.

As Celeste grew, so did Hinat's desire to worship in the cave. She would visit a couple of times a week, using the sacred water to bathe and prepare herself to speak to Spirit. Through the light of the sun which fell through the porthole, Hinat on occasion could almost see the symbols of information raining down, drying her in their rays, but also imparting knowledge and wisdom within her. Hinat realised that, as time passed, her abilities to scry in the sacred water became heightened and her knowing incredibly accurate. It was as if the combination of the cave, and her worship and hard work, had developed her sight and her abilities to a new level. She was known for her knowledge and strength when preparing binding spells and curse tablets, and her work grew steadily over time.

The temple was running smoothly and Hinat was able to develop her favourite pastime of scrying in the blood pool, as she had begun to call it. The water trickled in from the channel above, like a silent spiral of information, spinning around the edge of the pool's sides and base. It was crystal clear, reflecting the deep and beautiful colours of the rock below, and ensuring that the water spiral was almost invisible until, on occasion, the light would reflect from it and the movement would become apparent. Within this movement, the images that began to flow were intense and fascinating. It was as if Hinat was being shown a story, each visit being like a new chapter, with the same characters and images playing out their lives. Hinat did not always understand everything that she was seeing but she knew it was from a different world and time. What she did begin to understand was that this woman that she was able to glimpse and follow was her in another lifetime. It was a world which she didn't recognise but she could see that she would be cheated on and betrayed, and her anger and indignation intensified. As the images and different lifetimes showed the same repeating pattern, Hinat's emotions began to increase and pool, as if in a direct reflection of the blood pool in her world. As she continued to watch herself in many incarnations, she realised that she could access any point on her soul's journey across time and space and was completely awed by the realisation. Her soul, just like everyone's soul, could never be destroyed. It would travel across time, in different bodies and lives, but always the essence was the same and there was a common theme to all the lessons being learnt. Over and over again, she would be pushed to step into her own power and to truly believe in the immense energy that she was. The players and scenes may be different, but ultimately, she realised that the main intention of her soul was to grow and expand to its fullest potential.

It wasn't easy to watch at times, and on many occasions, Hinat would sit and sob at the images which flowed in front of her. Other times her heart would swell, and she felt proud of that self being able to achieve her fullest potential. However, Hinat was shown that she was not always going to be successful in her future lives. One particular future existence pulled at Hinat, and she vowed to help her future self if possible. If she did, she came to understand that the scales would tip in her favour, and she could move on to other lessons. If she could master this step, then she would not have to keep repeating it, and a whole new world of understanding and abilities would present themselves to her.

Hinat let the droplets run over her naked body, as she knelt by the gentle stream, cupping the cool water over her head and shoulders. It was so important for her to cleanse and purify her physical body before connecting with her other lives. As she stood, the droplets made interconnecting pathways down her back and limbs, like beautiful streams of light. Her stunning copper red hair now darkened, and the curls tightened, making a striking contrast to her skin.

Gently, Hinat stepped into the beam of light from the ceiling of the cave above, raising her face to the heat – which immediately began to dry her hair and skin with its intensity. She slowly knelt before the pool, looking intently into the dark red water, her long damp curls creating a concealing curtain around her face. Breathing slowly and deeply, Hinat set her intention to connect to her future life – which she had seen and connected to many times previously – and to talk to the new incarnation of herself. There was also another woman in that lifetime, an older woman who was incredibly powerful in her connection and use of Spirit, and Hinat could feel the intensity of their energies heighten whenever they were able to locate each other. There was also a man who Hinat knew she had met before, and who was repeating a negative pattern of behaviour. The man was weak in this lifetime and Hinat knew exactly how he could be stopped. Hinat could feel her fury whenever the man was mentioned or came into view. This time she had decided to do something about it. She knew exactly what spell to use, and what it would do to him. Hinat glanced around at the various items which she had carefully placed around the edge of the pool, ready to prepare the energetic magic and send it into her future incarnation. The dark energy must be released into the interconnecting portal between them, swirling and flowing into the man's energy, thickening it so that it slowed and eventually stopped. The man would be dealt with, and with that act, her future would be improved.

The Dark Stream

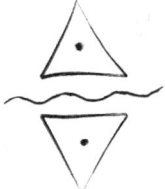

Joel felt angry as he made his way into his office building. An invisible dark cloud seemed to hang over him, causing him to have his head down, his shoulders hunched over, and a scowl etched across his forehead. He hadn't felt this angry for a long time but now the cloud had come back with a vengeance, bigger and darker than before. He knew this feeling and it scared him slightly. It never ended well. He started to expand his breathing slightly and slowly muttered under his breath. If anyone had been standing close to Joel, they would have heard him counting, a coping mechanism that he had learnt in the past to control the wave of menacing emotion trying to envelop him. After a few minutes of counting, as he rode the lift to his floor, he deliberately paused to check how he felt. The cloud was still there. In fact, it felt worse, and there was something else there that Joel had never felt before. He felt an ice-cold shiver go down his spine and he could not shake the feeling of doom that came over him.

He suddenly felt very frightened and had to steady himself slightly. He quickly made his way to his desk so that he could sit down.

'Would you like a coffee Mr Brooker-Jones?' one of the secretaries asked him as she made her way past his desk.

'Yes, please,' Joel managed, although the effort didn't stretch to a smile, just a grimace.

'Are you okay?' she asked, suddenly concerned for him. 'Are you in pain?' she bent slightly to peer into his face.

'I'm fine!' Joel snapped. 'Thanks for asking,' he added as he realised how sharp he had sounded.

'Okay, no problem,' she said as she made her way to the kitchen, glancing over her shoulder at him, clearly not convinced.

Joel sighed and gripped the edge of his desk slightly. That was the trouble with open-plan offices, there was no hiding certain things.

The day seemed to drag and everything seemed such an effort. His head pounded and he felt nauseous and weak. Joel was not sure he was getting much work done, and what he was doing never seemed to be finished. He realised that he needed to go home to try and sleep this feeling off. Once this decision had been made, he quickly stood up to leave, and completely blacked out.

The loud thud caused every head in the office to turn in Joel's direction, and those nearest to him rushed to his side. He lay outstretched and still on the cool ceramic tiles of the office floor, one arm raised above his head as if pointing to Ava, who stood at the side of her desk several rows away, a shocked expression on her face.

Cassie was having morning coffee with Sophia and Martha when her phone started to vibrate on the counter in front of her. She quickly moved to pick it up.

'Hello. Yes, that's me. Oh, my goodness, is he okay? Yes, of course. Okay, yes, I understand. What hospital is it? St. George's? Yes, okay, no problem. Thank you for phoning me. Bye.'

Sophia and Martha stood completely still during this conversation, frozen in their positions as they listened to only Cassie's side of the conversation.

'It's Joel,' Cassie said immediately, her glance stuck on Sophia. 'He collapsed at work. They've taken him to St. George's.'

Sophia did not move. Her eyes went from Cassie to Martha and then back again, her mouth slightly open and a shocked expression on her face. Her hand shook slightly and she put her cup down to stop it spilling.

'It's okay, I'll take you all in my car,' Martha instructed. 'I'll drive. Get your things together and let's get going.' Martha was halfway out of Sophia's back door as she said these words. 'I'm just getting my keys.'

Sophia and Cassie looked at each other and then without a word swung into action, collecting their bags, coats, and Xander, and making their way to the front door. The three met on the drive outside and the girls bundled into Martha's small but new little Ka Zetec. There was just enough room for all of them and they set off in silence to the famous old hospital where Joel had been taken.

As soon as they arrived, Cassie made her way to reception and was immediately directed around the corner to A&E, which had a separate entrance. Cassie's mind was whirring as they hurried around the building. She felt sick to her stomach and worried as to what had happened to Joel. He had not been himself of late, often looking tired and sweaty. She had enquired as to how he felt several times, but he had always just waved her away saying he was fine. Her mind kept going to the Magus, the image of her present in Cassie's mind's eye as if ever present in her life. Cassie's instinct told her that the Magus was responsible for this turn of events just as she had been shown, and she was suddenly more scared than angry. That means I am doing this to him, she thought with rising panic. But how do I stop it?

Eventually, Cassie and Sophia were led into the small, curtained cubicle in A&E where Joel was being seen. Martha sat in the reception area reading a book to Xander to distract him until his mum and grandmother returned.

Both Cassie and Sophia were shocked when they saw Joel. He was conscious but clearly still dopey. He was sweating profusely and the dark curls around his forehead were half stuck to him and half sticking up at angles. His breathing seemed laboured and rattled at times.

'We are doing all the tests we can, but we can't tell you what the cause is yet,' one of the doctors began to explain to Cassie. 'We are at a bit of a loss, to be honest. The only thing we have found is that his blood pressure is a bit high, but nothing else. We will keep you advised though,' and he patted her shoulder kindly as he exited the cubicle.

Cassie knew they wouldn't find anything of significance as the disruption wasn't in his physical body yet, it was in his energy field. She had done a lot of reading about the energy field of late and she knew that most physical illnesses developed because of emotions held in the energy field and not dealt with. Cassie had come to understand that these emotions, which people unconsciously stored in their energetic bodies following a life trauma, would eventually filter into the physical body if they weren't processed and released. Joel had a massive disruption in his energy field but it wasn't quite present yet in his physical, although it was beginning to filter in.

Cassie stood watching her husband, peering at him as if she could see the disruption getting closer to him. She felt strange. She wasn't as upset as she felt she should be. Too much water had gone under the bridge between them and the fact that he had betrayed her for so long, and so quickly after Xander's birth, had hardened her heart towards him. Cassie realised with a start that she felt empowered looking at her poorly and completely vulnerable husband lying in his hospital bed. She knew this was wrong and she certainly didn't want to kill him or even do him any more harm, but she felt that he was experiencing almost immediate karma and that made her feel justified and, to some extent, satisfied. From her reading, she knew that once people learned their lessons and the reason why something kept occurring in their lives, then the situation often disappeared. She wondered if Joel would know that this was her doing, or that he was experiencing karma because of his affair. It would be typical of Joel that the significance of the situation would go completely over his head.

Cassie gently rubbed Sophia's shoulder. She was sitting next to her son, holding his hand, and whispering encouragement into his ear. Cassie felt sorry for the concern and upset that Sophia was feeling, but she also knew that Sophia did not approve of Joel's behaviour and that she was very firmly on her side.

Eventually, the two ladies were gently told to leave as Joel was being taken to a ward and would need to get some rest. Joel had protested strongly at being told he would have to stay overnight. He just wanted to go home to his own bed, but the doctors were concerned with his sweating, high blood pressure, and poor breathing. They reassured him that if they could find nothing further, he would be allowed home the next day, and Sophia promised to come and collect him. Cassie deliberately said nothing, and it did not go unnoticed by Joel. His young wife was not rushing to collect him, and he wondered whether she wanted him back at all.

He watched Cassie as she had a conversation with one of the doctors, not listening to the words being spoken, but focusing on her face. She had lost weight of late, and with her hair pulled back in a messy ponytail with tendrils falling around her face, he realised how beautiful she was. It shocked him that he hadn't seen her properly in the past few months. She seemed to have changed as well; the way she looked people directly in the eyes when she spoke to them was reflective of a strong, confident woman. Joel felt a heaviness in his heart as he realised what a mess he had made of his life of late. If the affair had never happened, where would they be now? He felt suddenly very foolish as if he was the butt of a huge Universal joke, and his eyes pricked slightly as he fought back the tears.

'What are we going to do, Cassie? We must speak to the Magus,' Sophia whispered to her daughter-in-law as they made their way back to the reception area to find Martha and Xander.

Cassie looked slightly unnerved. 'Okay. Should I go and see Sara?'

'No. Martha will do it,' said Sophia, almost running to find her friend.

'Martha? What do you mean?' Cassie called after her, hurrying to keep up.

When the three ladies eventually got back to Cassie's home, Sophia and Martha quickly pulled together a small meal for them all whilst Cassie put Xander to bed. He had been totally exhausted by all the rushing around and Cassie had to keep him entertained in the car to stop him from falling asleep. However, now they were home, she was able to put him in his sleep suit and allow him to drift off. She watched him for a few minutes, her love for him swelling in her heart and the events of the day causing her to become quite emotional and shed a few tears. She stifled her sobs so as not to wake him but allowed the tears to finally flow. After a few minutes, she dried her face, blew her nose, and made her way downstairs.

It was obvious to Sophia and Martha that Cassie had been crying when she arrived in the kitchen, her eyes were red and moist, and she looked extremely tired.

'Oh, darling, don't worry. Joel is going to be fine, I promise you,' Sophia reassured her. 'Come and try and eat, you'll feel so much better for it,' and she motioned towards the table and the risotto which they had hurriedly thrown together.

'It looks lovely.' Cassie smiled and went to sit at the table with the other ladies. She realised that she was hungry and began to enjoy the meal that had been placed in front of her.

'That was delicious,' she said after she'd scraped her plate clean. 'Thank you both so much for your support today. It was much appreciated.' She looked at the two ladies who had also finished their meals and were just placing their cutlery on their empty plates.

'Now what is this about Martha being able to contact the Magus?'

Sophia quickly and excitedly recanted to Cassie the evening that she and Martha had experienced in her conservatory, when they had been able to speak to the Magus and discover quite a lot more information. Cassie was stunned that they had tried talking to the Magus in this way and equally impressed at the results.

'Do you think you can do the same again?' she asked Martha.

'I'm sure I can. We can certainly have a go, can't we? It will be interesting to have you there as well. We will be talking to an aspect of you, and yet you'll be in the room. It's a bit mind-boggling, to be honest,' she concluded.

'I'm completely mind-boggled about all this,' Sophia said raising her hands in a gesture of confusion, and they all chuckled.

'It certainly is an unusual scenario,' Cassie agreed, 'but equally fascinating as well, and I love her name: the Red Magus.'

Sophia and Martha nodded in agreement and then quickly explained to Cassie how they had set up the room before with the candles and crystals. However, this time they all decided that they should sit around the dining table, so the two older women finished cleaning the table and set out some candles while Cassie began to collect a few items to use in the central space. As she looked around, her eyes landed on the glass cabinet in the sitting room, and she realised that she could use the knife. She gingerly took it from the cabinet and placed it in the centre of the table.

'I don't know why we need to use this but I think it's relevant,' she said. Sophia and Martha looked at her quizzically and Cassie began to explain to them the intense feeling that she had around the knife and that she believed it was the one that her brother had used to kill her in that other life. 'I think Matteo is Joel,' she said, abruptly ending her dialogue.

Neither Sophia nor Martha took their eyes off Cassie as they both slipped onto a dining room chair on either side of the table.

'I didn't realise there was another life involved,' Martha said. 'So, in that lifetime, Joel or Matteo killed you, and in this lifetime, you have the upper hand, so to speak.'

'If I don't want this cycle and this relationship to keep reoccurring, I have to stop this once and for all, don't I?' Cassie asked. Without waiting for a reply, she carried on, 'So, to stop the cycle I must save him this time. In that way, there will be no need for revenge or a further replay of the situation.'

'Exactly!' Martha said. 'You're right. You want to end the need for retaliation or revenge, cut that cycle off so that you can go on to another lesson. If you do that, all the negative energy from the situation which has been held in your soul will be released.'

'I like the idea of that,' Cassie replied, smiling at them both. 'Are you okay Sophia?' she asked. Her mother-in-law had been very quiet and Cassie realised this must be difficult for her.

'Yes, dear, I'm fine,' Sophia smiled and nodded at her. 'Just mesmerised by the whole conversation. What I don't understand though is that you, as Cassie, don't want to hurt Joel, but you as the Magus does. How does that work?' and she looked from Cassie to Martha and back again.

Cassie smiled thoughtfully, 'Any ideas, Martha?' she said.

Martha thought for a few minutes and then said, 'I believe that the actions of the Magus are yours but at an unconscious level. I think you are probably very angry – which I could feel when I spoke to the Magus before. In fact, she was livid and was adamant that she was not going to endure this same cycle repeatedly. I believe those are your feelings somewhere, whether you are conscious of them or not, but the strength of them will become overpowering.' She leant towards Cassie, looking at her straight in the eyes and holding her gaze for a few seconds. 'You, Cassie, are extremely powerful energetically and I believe that everything we are doing and moving towards is so that you remember your real purpose in this current life.'

There was a long silence as Martha's words settled slowly around them.

Cassie hung her head as she said, 'Yes, you are right about the anger. I didn't feel it at first, I just felt lost and hurt, but it's been getting stronger and stronger. If the power of the Magus is because of our joint anger, then I must release that. I wonder if I'm also extremely angry at my own childhood as well as my brother in the Roman life. Maybe it's about the accumulation of anger over all three lifetimes?' She looked up at her companions for their agreement.

'Yes, I agree,' Martha said, nodding. 'I wonder if there are many other lives in which you have been killed or betrayed. I wonder if that is a lesson that you have been learning and that the accumulation of many streams of anger is what is giving the Magus, or you, the power to affect Joel's energy. Maybe Joel's soul has been involved in all those lifetimes and therefore what is happening is like a major conclusion for you both on many levels.'

'Gosh!' Cassie exclaimed, 'I'm a bit nervous now,' and she took Sophia's hand for comfort. Sophia rubbed it gently as she struggled to follow the conversation.

'The question is,' Martha said, ignoring Cassie's last comment, 'how do we release all that anger? If it's so strong that it's affecting Joel's energy, we can't just redirect it somewhere else, it would do harm there as well. Where do we send it and how?'

'Shall I ring Sara?' Cassie asked. 'She knows so much about past lives – maybe she will be able to help us.'

Martha nodded, 'That's a brilliant idea. I'm sure she'll have some useful suggestions.' Cassie had already picked up her phone.

Unfortunately, Cassie only got Sara's answer machine, so the three women busied themselves finishing the table display with the pocketknife, a selenite heart that Joel had given Cassie one year and which seemed pertinent to the situation, and a rainbow candle which Cassie had bought on their last holiday. Martha then helped them both to connect to their breath and to expand their energy, grounding both themselves and the room. Even if Sara didn't get back in touch this evening it didn't hurt to connect in and set their intention. Both Cassie and Sophia felt themselves relaxing more and more over the course of the next hour or so, and although Sara didn't phone them back, they both felt ready to get a good night's sleep.

Just as they were finishing their mediation, a thought occurred to Cassie. 'What should I do about the effigy?' she asked the others.

'What effigy?' Martha asked slightly confused.

Cassie looked from one to the other and suddenly realised that she hadn't told them about the little wax figure. When she had finished, Martha and Sophia sat with open mouths. It was a full few minutes before either of them dared to speak. 'I am dumbfounded!' Martha exclaimed. 'How could you forget that!'

Cassie looked a bit concerned. 'Well, I wasn't sure how to use it, so I suppose I put it to the back of my mind, and then with Joel being ill and everything…'

'Can we see it?' Martha asked quietly. 'I have never seen an apport and I would love to. I think it's very significant to how we conclude this matter, to be honest.'

Cassie went upstairs to fetch the little package. When she returned, she gently placed it in the middle of the table between them. She gingerly pulled on the string holding the package together and, as she tugged, the four corners of the material fell away to reveal the little figure lying on its side in the middle. Both older ladies put on their glasses and slowly leant forward to examine the figure.

'I find it a little creepy,' Sophia eventually offered.

'Yes, me too,' Cassie said patting her hand. 'I think that's why I haven't done anything with it.'

'And this just appeared out of thin air?' Martha exclaimed again, poking her finger towards the figure.

Cassie solemnly nodded whilst Martha leant even closer, examining every detail of the wax figure.

'Well,' she finally said, 'I'm stunned but fascinated as well. I really think we should do something with it if the Magus gave it to you. I think it's the catalyst for the whole process.'

'Okay,' Cassie said, 'but I'll have to bring Sara and Alice in to help if that's okay with you both.'

'Of course,' Sophia and Martha chimed together.

'This is your spell after all,' Martha added.

'I'll leave the table set up as it is and as soon as Sara comes back, I'll let you know,' Cassie informed Sophia and Martha as they put on their coats and prepared to leave. They were all very tired now and needed a good night's sleep before they attempted to speak to the Magus and do what they needed to do. They had a lovely group hug before making their way back to their individual beds to sleep and recharge.

Cassie had slept deeply and had woken around 5 a.m. refreshed and ready for what was to come. She and Xander were already up the next morning, enjoying coffee – in Cassie's case – and some breakfast – in Xander's – when Cassie's mobile phone rang.

'Hi Sara, thanks for coming back to me. How are you?'

'I'm good thanks. I got your message but to be honest I didn't really understand it. What did you need help with?'

Cassie explained to Sara, as best she could, the conclusion that she, Sophia and Martha had come to the previous night, the situation with Joel, and how she needed to break the cycle and bring these situations to a close.

'Gosh, that's so interesting!' Sara exclaimed when Cassie had finished speaking. 'So, what you need to do now is decide how you can release the anger and help Joel to recover. Is that right?'

'Yes. We wondered if you could come and help us. Martha is going to try and speak to the Red Magus again with us all there and see whether she can help us, and we need to work out how to use the effigy. I know that the Red Magus is part of me, but I don't seem to have access to her in the same way that Martha does.'

'Well, I suppose Martha is more detached from the situation and therefore it's easier for her. Yes, of course, I'll help. Just text me some dates and times and we'll sort something out. I'm excited to be part of it, so thank you, and I know Alice will be as well.'

Cassie spent the next couple of hours liaising with them all to confirm dates and times and eventually had a get-together written in her diary. They had wanted to make it as soon as possible as they were all very conscious that Joel was suffering and that this needed to be resolved. Just as Cassie had marked the meeting on her calendar the phone went again letting her know that Joel could come home whenever someone could pick him up. Cassie rang Sophia immediately and she and Patrick said that they would go that day. Sophia suggested that Joel stay with them for a while as they would have more time to care for him, rather than placing that burden on Cassie. Cassie was very grateful for her kind suggestion, knowing that it was probably a good idea to have some distance between them for a while. She was aware of her own anger towards Joel, which had been building steadily over the last few weeks, growing and intensifying. She had always remained calm, hiding her true feelings from everyone, but she was scared that they would explode for all to see. She knew that Joel would be pampered by his parents and would enjoy chatting with his mum and dad every day, which irritated her further in a way. They had always been a very close family and it would do him good to have them around, but why should he have that comfort? She gratefully agreed to the idea of the separation, however, and breathed a long sigh of relief as she put the phone down.

Cassie spent the rest of the day doing normal cleaning and washing tasks, enjoying the mundane routine for once in her life. There was nothing weird and wonderful about her hanging out washing or preparing her son's lunch. The normality of it was greatly welcomed for the first time in her life.

Talking To The Magus

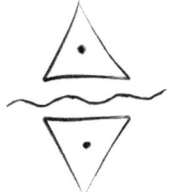

Sophia and Patrick had collected their son that day and brought him home. His old childhood room had long ago been redecorated and turned into a study, so he was now ensconced in the newly decorated guest room on the ground floor, at the back of their house. It meant that he didn't need to climb the stairs, which he was finding difficult, and had easy access to the downstairs toilet and shower room. It also meant that he had a little privacy. These arrangements seemed to be working well. However, Joel's condition was not improving. He was incredibly fatigued and struggled to get out of bed most days. He was constantly sweating profusely, so much so that Sophia needed to change his sheets almost every day. A task that she did gladly for her son, but the unchanging symptoms worried her, and she almost counted the minutes until they could talk to the Red Magus again. Of course, she did not breathe a word of their plans or anything that had gone before, to either Patrick or Joel.

They would probably both think she was completely crazy, and sometimes she wondered if she was. It was all so fanciful but paradoxically there was clearly something going on. There was just too much information to suggest otherwise.

Just before the planned meeting with Cassie, Martha, Sara and Alice, Sophia decided to question her son a little more about his behaviour and what had been going on in his marriage. After all, what could he do or say to her in his condition? He was so weak that he had no energy to really become angry and she intuitively felt that a conversation would be of assistance.

As she finished changing the sheets that morning and putting them into the washing machine, she made them both a coffee and set the mugs on a small tray. Next to them she placed a glass of water and measured out Joel's blood pressure medication, and some herbal supplements that had been recommended to her. She had checked with the doctor that they wouldn't interfere with the traditional medicine that he was taking and had been given the all-clear. Sophia felt as if the doctors were at a bit of a loss as to what was going on, so could see no harm in the additional complementary help. Picking up the tray, she headed into the guest room to talk to her son. She silently placed the tray on the table next to the bed and then handed him the glass of water in one hand and the pills in the other. He took them without a word and swigged back the medication, handing the glass back to his mother once he had taken a few gulps. Sophia leant forward to plump up the large pillows behind him as he sat propped up in his bed and, once he was comfortable, handed him his coffee. She then settled down with hers in the tall wing-backed chair which Patrick had brought in for her, for exactly this reason

– so that she could sit and talk to Joel or just be with him while he slept.

Joel looked rough. His skin was very pale and his dark curls constantly looked damp from the sweating. The doctors had advised that this was a common reaction to the body being unsettled and trying to recalibrate, and there was really nothing they could do about it.

'Could you just get me a fresh T-shirt, Mum?' Joel asked, pulling at the front of the one he had on. 'This feels damp again.' Sophia got up and found a clean one, handing it to her son as he changed without moving from the bed. The old one was placed in the dirty laundry bin next to the bedroom door, ready for washing.

'Thanks,' Joel muttered as he slumped back against the pillow, the exertion of changing his top almost too much to cope with.

'Joel,' Sophia started, 'I wanted to ask you something. I know this might not be easy and not something you would usually chat to me about, but I do think in the circumstances that you need to be honest with me.' She leant forward slightly, looking him directly in the eyes. 'I want to know what has been going on with this red-haired woman.'

Joel held his mother's gaze, completely taken aback by her forceful tone. He was very surprised by the unexpected questioning. How did she know that Ava had red hair? Usually, she wouldn't enquire about anything personal or if she did, he would easily bat her away with his comments and just avoid telling her anything. This time, however, he just didn't have the energy and, in some way, he felt like he needed to get everything off his chest. Maybe the way he felt had to do with the guilt that he carried, and that by clearing it he would start to feel better. He had no idea, but his instinct was to come completely clean.

'I've been an idiot, Mum,' he said. His large hazel eyes swelled with tears. 'I'm so sorry,' the words caught in his throat. Sophia's heart nearly broke seeing her son so vulnerable and upset but she knew that she had to stay strong with him.

'Yes, you have,' she said nodding her head and gently rubbing his hand. 'Start from the beginning so I can understand.'

Joel did as she asked. He explained about the effect Ava had on him and the affair that had begun. He told Sophia about the feelings he had for Cassie whilst she was suffering after the birth of Xander and how he knew they were selfish, but that he just couldn't fully understand what she was experiencing, and it made him feel like a failure as a husband. In turn, he felt angry with her and that had pushed him into the affair. Surprisingly, he also found himself telling his mother about the dark thoughts he had about getting rid of Cassie, and how they had shocked and sickened him, but also how they had felt familiar and comforting as well. Something that he had not understood, and still didn't.

Sophia was terribly upset by the whole story, although she tried not to show it, and equally shocked at this dark revelation. Of course, she also had additional information and could begin to see that those memories had felt comforting and familiar to Joel, or Matteo, because he had killed Cassie in another life. The familiarity was a memory locked somewhere in his energy field, and it felt comforting as he recognised it, even if the life that it came from was not pleasant and didn't end well. Although she was glad that Joel had purged everything he had done and felt to her, she was ashamed of his behaviour and for the first time, she told him that. Part of her struggled to say those words to her son when he was at his lowest, but part of her felt very liberated that she could be so honest and blunt with him. Joel was shocked and hurt by his mother's reaction, but equally could understand her viewpoint, and was proud of her for her strength.

'I know I've behaved in a terrible way,' he said, wiping a few tears from his face, 'but I want to make amends to Cassie, Xander, you and Dad. You're all my family. You're a good mum and I want to make you all proud of me again.'

Sophia's heart ached but she stayed as calm as she could. 'I'm glad to hear that, Joel. I love you dearly and I just want you to be happy. I'm not sure Cassie will take you back now though, but you still need to be there for them both. I want you to continue with the counselling sessions, and I want you to learn some major lessons from this experience.'

Joel nodded at her, feeling like a small child being scolded by his mother, which in a way he was.

The conversation had been exhausting for them both and Joel quickly fell asleep, so Sophia quietly left her son and went to lie down too. Her head and chest ached from all the emotion and she felt drained. She didn't usually nap during the day but she hadn't been sleeping well and the events of the morning had taken their toll. She was asleep as soon as her head hit the pillow.

Sophia felt extremely apprehensive as she showered and dressed in readiness for the meeting with the others. They had decided to hold it at Sara's, a neutral venue and away from Joel residing in Sophia's guest room. Patrick had agreed to babysit for Xander, and Cassie had dropped him at their house early, once he was fed and bathed, so that she could go home and get ready with a clear head and no distractions. Patrick and Xander were in the shed at that moment, playing with the figures that Patrick used for his battle scenes. The two of them were having great fun together, and Patrick thoroughly enjoyed having Xander to himself occasionally. Both women were able to fully relax knowing that Xander's grandad was in charge for the evening, and fully capable of caring for his beloved grandson.

Sophia slowly dressed in loose, comfortable, patterned trousers and a matching plain jersey top. She wanted to feel comfortable and relaxed for this experience, whatever it would bring. She had absolutely no idea what was going to happen or be revealed, and the lack of knowing was making her very anxious. She realised that she was also very excited at this turn of events. She had felt completely out of her comfort zone over the last few months but she was also fascinated that any of this even existed. How did I get to my age with no idea about energy work? she thought to herself.

Sophia looked in the gold-framed, full-length mirror in her room and liked what she saw. She was over sixty now but she was still trim and petite, and although her sense of style had changed gradually to accommodate her age, she still looked stylish and on-trend. Her dark curly hair had been cut quite short this time, and as it framed her face, a few curls escaped around the edge and accentuated her Mediterranean features. Of course, the edges were now full of white, but this provided a soft frame to her face and only seemed to highlight her skin in a forgiving way. Sophia had been a beautiful woman in her youth and although the years had aged her, she still was. She finished her outfit with some dark grey, drop pearl earrings and a matching seed pearl bracelet. With a few squirts of perfume, she was ready for the evening and what it might bring. A slight smile momentarily lit up her face.

Once downstairs, she knocked gently on Joel's bedroom door. Receiving no response, she carefully stuck her head around it. The room was dark, with just a gentle glow from the bedside lamp, and she could see that Joel was fast asleep. She paused for a moment, listening to the sound of his breathing and hearing a regular gentle breath. She quietly pulled the door shut, thinking that it was perhaps good that he was asleep. If the Magus was able to reverse the process tonight, it would probably be better if he was unaware of what was happening. Little did she know, however, that Joel was going to take an active role in the evening's proceedings.

Grabbing a torch from beside the back door, which was left exactly for this reason, Sophia navigated her way to her husband's favourite place – the garden shed. The glow from the window illuminated the bottom half of the garden so well that she was able to turn off her torch halfway to her destination. 'I'm off,' she said as she pushed open the creaky wooden door. Patrick was sitting on the other side of a huge table which was basically the size of the shed with only a narrow walkway around each side. Xander was on his lap. They were both totally enthralled with the scene on the table: a landscape strewn with figures, tanks, and the like. They both looked up in unison as Sophia entered and she had to chuckle at the sight of them. 'I'm off out with Cassie. I'll be back late so don't wait up for me.'

'No problem,' Patrick smiled at her, 'we're having great fun here, aren't we munchkin?' He directed his last comment to

Xander and ruffled his hair. 'Look, we've got a great stash of chocolate raisins,' and he shook a small tin that was perched on a shelf behind him.

Sophia smiled, 'Just don't make him sick, will you?'

'Don't be daft. Have a good time, by the way, and be careful.' Patrick looked up at her seriously for a moment.

His face made her stop in her tracks for a second. Sometimes Sophia thought he had no idea about what was going on in their lives, and other times she thought he knew everything and could see into her very soul.

'Of course,' she smiled, 'have fun you two.'

Cassie pulled up on the drive a few minutes later, and Martha appeared instantaneously as she did so. She must have been ready and watching out for them, Sophia thought as she hugged her friend in welcome. Martha carefully got into the back seat behind Cassie, and Sophia sat in the front as they set off en route to Sara's. Once arrived they were warmly welcomed and ushered into Sara's treatment room, where Sara had set up a large white table and chairs for their arrival. The three ladies stood to the side of the room as they took in the scene. Sara had created a crystal grid on the floor around the table, taking up most of the space, with only a small area near the doorway free of crystals. The grid consisted of intricate interlocking geometric patterns with rows of little tumbled crystals making up each of the sides. The crystals were all different colours and shapes but all quite small, so the effect was of a mesmerising pattern on the floor. In the four corners of the room were free-standing black metal sconces, on which she had lit four large white candles, the soft glow causing the crystals to glisten and create an almost moving field of light.

'Gosh,' Cassie said, 'this looks beautiful.'

They all nodded in unison, their faces lit up by the crystal light.

'It must have taken you ages,' Sophia added.

'It did. Come and sit down – but be careful,' Sara said as she tiptoed through the crystals to take a seat at the table. The others carefully followed. To one side of the table, within reach of Sara, was another, narrow and smaller table on which was a jug of water and five glasses, some incense and matches, and a notepad and pen.

'If any of you want a drink of water just let me know. I've tried to think of everything we might need, so we don't have to keep getting up. I thought we needed lots of protection,' Sara said as she gestured to the crystal grid around them. 'Crystals will facilitate communication with other dimensions but will also protect us from anything negative.' The group nodded in understanding.

'What's that one?' Martha asked, scanning the crystals and landing on a series of beautiful grey ones which almost seemed to contain their own colours and light. 'They are stunning, as if they have lights inside.'

'That's labradorite,' Sara explained, 'it is beautiful, isn't it? It's an amazing protector. I've included quite a few of them in the grid on all sides.'

'It's really lovely,' Cassie said as she scanned the crystals, swivelling in her chair to do so. 'Really stunning and very powerful as well, I should think.'

'Exactly,' Sara said with emphasis. 'I think we need lots of support and protection tonight. We will set our intention as a group to only speak to the Red Magus and that nothing that is without love and light will come through into the room.'

'Alice should be here soon. Do you have the effigy?' Sara asked Cassie.

Cassie nodded and put her hand into one of the small pockets of her handbag. She pulled out the little package which she placed in the centre of the table, and gently pulled the string open again to reveal the figure. Sara set about encircling it with crystals.

'I've also brought a few extra items,' Cassie said and pulled out the selenite heart, rainbow candle and the penknife which she had previously gathered, after Joel had been taken ill. As she finished arranging the items, the doorbell went, and Sara vanished to let Alice in. Once they had all hugged each other in welcome, and Alice had been introduced to Martha and Sophia, Sara set up the diffuser with a blend of myrrh, elemi, and iris.

'I've added iris as well,' she said to the room in general. 'It just felt right to do so. It's the national flower of Jordan and is used to help transition souls who are confused. I thought the connection was significant, and it can't hurt.' Sara shrugged her shoulders. As she finished speaking, she turned off the main light, allowing the soft glow of the candles to encircle them. It felt very atmospheric and the small group sat in silence for a while enjoying the twinkling crystals and the beautiful scent.

'So, how do we start this?' Sophia asked after a few minutes. The women looked towards Sara for an answer.

'Well, I think that we begin with some breathing exercises.

Martha can help us to open up our energy, ground the room and protect ourselves, and then set our mutual intention,' Sara looked at Martha for agreement.

'Yes, sounds good to me,' Martha nodded in agreement. 'Before we start, how should we use the effigy?' she said directing her question at Alice who sat wide-eyed opposite her.

'Well, I think we should put the effigy in a stone bowl for a start so we can burn it. I think we need to write Joel's girlfriend's name on a piece of paper, or on the cloth that it was wrapped in, and burn it as well to release the spell. By naming the woman we will direct the energy of the spell towards her.'

'Okay. Everyone agrees?' The others nodded and Sara got up, carefully tiptoeing through the crystals to fetch a stone bowl as directed. She came back with a pretty earthenware cream bowl, seemingly dipped in a dark green glaze around the rim. She gently placed the cloth in front of Cassie, and then positioned the herbs, string, and effigy in the bowl and set a box of matches next to it.

'I think you need to write the name on the cloth,' she said to Cassie, handing her a black marker pen.

Cassie pulled the cloth towards her and carefully wrote the word AVA on one side. 'Sorry, did you say we should burn the cloth as well or place it under the bowl?' she asked looking at Alice for assistance.

'I think it will need to be burnt eventually, but you could place it under the bowl while we burn the rest, so it's clear who the spell is intended for. That might be a better way,' Alice answered.

'Okay,' Cassie said and carefully spread the little square of cloth out flat, placing the bowl and its contents on top. Once finished, Sara rearranged the crystals around the edge and placed some extra little tea lights in glass holders to join them.

'I think we should cleanse the area first,' Martha added, motioning towards Sara. Sara took an incense stick and wafted the sweet-smelling smoke around the bowl arrangements and then around the room to cleanse the space of any negative energy that did not need to be present at that time.

Sara spoke next. 'Then we can let Martha connect with her guides and see whether we can call in the Red Magus again. Cassie, I suggest that you take your awareness to your heart and solar plexus whilst Martha is doing that, to strengthen the connection if possible.'

Cassie nodded intently.

'Are we ready, ladies?' Sara asked, smiling at them all.

'Just before we start,' Martha interrupted, 'I don't know why this is relevant, but can I tell you all about my dream?' She looked at them all a little sheepishly. 'I'm just getting the feeling that I should.'

'Yes, go for it, Martha,' Sara said.

They all listened intently whilst Martha explained about the crow and the significance of the bird in spiritual terms.

'I've seen the bird as well,' Cassie said. 'I was aware of the bird in the cave but the Magus didn't shapeshift. She was washing herself and talking to someone. I couldn't hear anything but I knew that information was being exchanged.'

'It's so interesting, isn't it, how she is getting information to us,' Sara looked around at the circle of fascinated faces. 'Okay, let's begin. Martha?'

Martha nodded and gently took them through the process of relaxing through breath, balancing themselves and grounding the room in their mind's eye. They then set their intention to speak to the Red Magus and for only the Red Magus to come through, for the highest good of all of them present. Martha also added that they were to find a compromise between those parts of Cassie that would lead to healing and expansion for both Cassie and Joel, and that any karmic patterning could once and for all be released between them. Finally, she asked that all parts of Cassie and Joel be integrated back into the whole.

Once this was completed, Martha closed her eyes, gently taking herself to a space in which she could talk to her guides and call on the Red Magus. As she did so, Sara quietly handed out glasses of water, lit some more incense, and got the notepad ready in case she needed to jot any information down. Once settled, the four waited in silence for Martha to speak.

It seemed a long time before Martha spoke but when she did, it was almost as if someone else was talking. Her voice was deep and resonant and the others were slightly startled. Sara jotted on the notepad and pushed it over to the others so that they could see the page.

'She's channelling her guide' it said, and the others nodded without really understanding what that meant. All four held their breath waiting for Martha to continue.

'The Red Magus is coming to speak to you tonight. She would very much like to communicate with you and for this karmic cycle to be released and brought to an end. I can see her now. She is here, ready. Martha is to speak to her. I am here if you need me,' Martha's guide concluded.

When Martha spoke again, it was in her usual voice. 'I can see the Red Magus. What would you like to ask her?'

Cassie and Sophia looked at each other, slightly startled, but Cassie quickly pulled herself together and said, 'What are you doing to Joel?'

'She is saying that she is filling his energy field with all the anger that has been held in yours for life after life, as you have been betrayed and killed repeatedly. She has sent the anger from all those lives to him in order that he can feel what you have felt. Your joint anger is stagnating his energy and causing it to spike and break.'

The room was silent for a few moments before Martha said, 'I can see a queue behind her.'

'What do you mean, a queue?' Sara asked, instantly remembering the session with Cassie.

'Well, there is a long line of characters, presumably from many lives, standing behind her. All different women in different clothes and from different cultures. I think they are all from Cassie's different lives.'

'We've seen this, haven't we,' Cassie said. 'Can you describe any of them?'

'Well, it looks like there's a nun, a shaman, a woman in what looks like Victorian dress. They just go on and on. I knew you were an old soul, Cassie, but there's quite a few characters here.' Martha smiled gently.

'Can you ask the Magus what will happen to Joel eventually, please?' Cassie asked, bringing them back to the task at hand.

There was silence for a couple of minutes as Martha silently asked the question in her mind and waited for an answer.

'Death,' she said eventually, with no softening of the message. 'Joel will die if it continues but I don't think the Magus wants that. I think she wants to show him what she can do. What the anger of so many can do and that you can never beat karma in the end. If you kill repeatedly, you will be killed eventually.'

'An eye for an eye,' Sara added.

'Exactly,' Martha replied.

'So, when will she stop?' Cassie asked.

Again, there was silence for a couple of minutes. Then, 'I'm not sure.' Martha appeared hesitant for the first time. 'I can see Joel! He's come into the space. I think it's his highest self, come to take part in this meeting if you like, to negotiate with the Magus.' She sounded shocked as she said this, as they all were.

'I've never heard of this but why not? Presumably, if we are clearing the karmic patterns between Cassie and Joel, then his highest self will know about it and want to be part of it,' Sara concluded. 'Does he want to say anything?' she asked.

'He wants to apologise for his behaviour not only in this lifetime but over many, many lives. He is apologising to each character in the queue. He now understands that with this experience in this lifetime, he has been able to see the bigger picture of his actions and to understand the overall lessons that have taken place across these many lives. He is aware that this understanding will release the negative emotions which he has held from these lives, and that by doing so, his energy will be cleansed and expand.'

There was silence as these words settled around the room and the other four watched Martha, spellbound.

'As his energy can expand, he is aware that his soul will rise to another level of understanding and learning. Like another level of a spiral. He is extremely grateful for you, Cassie. You two have a soul bond, a promise at a soul level to help each other grow and develop. I think this lifetime is the culmination of a cycle of learning for you both over many lives. You will always be connected and will always love and help each other, although maybe in different guises. We all incarnate with a group of souls that have agreed to come to help us in this way. We all agreed to help you at a soul level, and we will again. All of us in this room are connected as well.' The women all smiled at each other.

'That's lovely and very comforting,' Sophia said.

Cassie nodded and they could see that she was very emotional and trying not to cry. 'Ignore me,' she said, shaking her head.

'Don't be silly. This was always going to be emotional. We are all receiving a massive learning, and that will release energy in the form of emotions. Cry if you need to, it is only energy being released and that's a good thing,' said Sara, patting Cassie's hand.

Cassie nodded silently with gratitude, gently biting her lip to stem the emotions flooding to the surface. Lifetimes of emotion wanting to be released.

Sophia took Cassie's hand as well to lend her support. 'Will Joel recover now?' she asked, still understandably concerned for her son in this lifetime.

'Yes, eventually. Now that he has apologised, Cassie can release the anger that has been held from her many lives, and therefore it is no longer directed at Joel. I think it will take a bit of time for it to be released but yes, he will get better,' Sara replied.

Sophia's shoulders dropped and she realised she had held a high level of tension throughout the whole evening. She finally found herself relaxing a little deeper for the first time in a long time, and she let out a gentle sigh. 'Thank goodness. That really is a weight off my mind.' The others nodded, fully understanding how difficult this had been for her, and grateful for her relief.

'Is there anything else the Magus would like to tell us?' Sara asked gently, bringing the focus back to Martha.

'She seems to have relaxed herself. She is smiling and I think she is happy about this happening. Joel and the queue have gone now and it's just her standing here. She really is beautiful and slightly scary as well. She has so much power in her.' Martha paused while she received a little more information. 'She wants to show us something.'

'What is it?' Cassie asked, trying to get her head around the fact that this woman Martha was describing was in fact an aspect of her. How could that be? Could she have been so powerful energetically once upon a time and, if so, how could she tap back into that?

'She's showing me scenes from her life. I wish you could all see this. Why don't you all close your eyes and see what comes to you in your mind's eye? I think she is going to show this to all of us.'

The others looked at each other in surprise but closed their eyes and focused on their third eye area. It slowly began to feel warm to each of them and, as it did, scenes flickered in front of them. At the end of the evening, they were able to compare their visions and realised that the Magus had indeed shown them all identical scenes of her life and her power.

'Wow,' said Sara. 'I'm not usually shocked but that was incredible! Did she shapeshift at one point?'

'Yes! Yes, she did,' Cassie exclaimed. 'That's certainly what it looked like. Into a crow just like in Martha's dream.'

'Yes, it was a crow. I wonder if that was literally or some sort of metaphor – like, although she had a tough life as a woman in those times, her spiritual beliefs allowed her to be free. What do you think?' Martha questioned.

'Maybe,' Sara said, 'that's a lovely explanation.'

'Who was she talking to in that cave?' asked Sophia.

'Yes, that was interesting, wasn't it?' Martha responded. 'It was obviously some underground cave, with the light coming through a portal at the top. She was definitely talking to someone above her, but I'm not sure who. What did you get Sara?'

Sara paused and looked at them all. 'Well, this is going to sound a bit fanciful,' she paused and laughter filled the room. 'What?' Sara exclaimed. 'Why are you laughing?' She joined in the laughter.

'All of this is so out there that I'm sure nothing else is going to shock us,' Cassie said.

'Well, yes, that's true,' Sara agreed, and they all chuckled again.

'What were you going to say?' Martha asked once the laughter had died down.

'Have you ever heard of the Sirius Star legend?' Sara began. The four ladies shook their heads. 'Well, very basically, there is a tribe in Mali called the Dogon who have very ancient pictures on their cave walls depicting a different race coming to earth, and they had information about the Sirius star that was only discovered much later by astrologers and confirmed accurate. The legend is that this other race, the Nommos, came down to earth and educated the tribespeople about the Sirius Star. I know it sounds weird but that's what came to my mind, that she was talking to people from Sirius.' Sara shrugged her shoulders as she finished this explanation and looked at the others.

'I felt she was talking to a star, but I didn't really understand what that meant,' Martha said. Then added, 'But I didn't get any more.'

'We will have to discover more about the Magus in some extra sessions. What do you think?' Sara looked at Cassie.

'Oh, my goodness, yes! I think we have a lot to learn about her.' Cassie felt very excited about the prospect.

'I think you should write it all down, Cassie. She was a fascinating character and it would be an amazing story.' Martha prompted.

'Yes, that's an idea. Maybe I will. Thank you so much, Martha, and everyone for your help and support.' Cassie paused and then said quietly, 'I wonder how Joel is feeling?'

The five ladies all looked at each other, each hoping that he would be feeling better.

'Now let's burn this sucker!' Cassie pulled the stoneware bowl towards her, striking a match and placing it to the little effigy. As the figure of the woman melted and lost its shape, morphing into a dirty white mass, a plume of grey smoke rose in an ever-increasing spiral towards the ceiling, as if energetically unravelling and releasing the elements of the spell into the Universe. The circle of five watched intently until the bowl contained only a puddle of wax, all of them seemingly transfixed. Eventually, Cassie pulled the square of fabric from under the bowl, and laid it over the wax, striking another match and watching as the flames took hold. This time the smoke was black and the cloth burned quickly until nothing remained.

Joel tossed and turned, his level of anxiety affecting his ability to sleep. He was dreaming fitfully, dropping into vivid imagery followed by periods of deeper dreamless sleep, yet his anxiety kept bringing him back to the disturbing scenes. He was in that battle again, the sun glaring, the men screaming, and it always ended with the image of the wound running down his arm. However, this time the wound was longer, running down his hand and between his fingers, almost severing his hand in half, and he realised that it was him screaming in fear and pain. He woke suddenly, breathing heavily and still sweating. He rolled over onto his side, pushing the covers off him in an effort to cool down. He closed his eyes again, drifting down into a period of rest.

In the next dream he was a soldier again, but this time the uniform was different. He was standing in a dark cavernous room, which felt as if it was underground. It felt damp and cold. In front of him was a metal cage and he could see a woman cowering at the back of it, crouching in the corner to appear as small as possible. Her clothes were dirty and her long curly hair was matted and damp, sticking to her head. He kicked the edge of the cage, making it shake. 'Filthy witch!!' he snarled at her. The woman's stance changed slightly. It was a tiny shift that many would not have seen, but it changed her whole energy and presence. She looked up, through the dark strands of red hair, her large clear eyes narrowing as she stared in defiance at the soldier in front of her. The soldier stepped back slightly, again a tiny movement but enough to show he was intimidated, before kicking the cage again and walking away into the darkness. The Magus relaxed, curling into a ball on the floor to rest, but the anger inside her did not rest and she knew she would have her revenge.

In the next dream, Joel could see faces close to him, peering at him with disdain. The faces of Cassie and his mother, Martha, and even old university friends, pressed close to his face and then faded into the darkness. It was unsettling. Ava's face also came into view, her features solemn and seemingly disappointed in him. Joel felt small in that instant, small and alone. He drifted again into the darkness.

The Healing

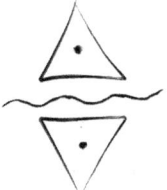

Following their incredible encounter with the Red Magus, and once the effigy had been fully burned, the group helped Sara pick up all the crystals and then made their way to her treatment room for some refreshments. Sara had laid out some nibbles and wine and the small group settled down for a thorough analysis of the evening. Of course, the topic of conversation eventually spread to their own lives, and they were still chatting as Sara's fun little cuckoo clock sounded midnight.

The next morning, Sophia woke late. She had slept soundly and was surprised to see it was almost ten when she finally opened her eyes. She could not remember dreaming at all but had seemed to sink into a deep space. She felt refreshed, and as the images of the night before came back to her, she also felt shocked. She climbed out of bed and made her way to the kitchen where she found Patrick reading the newspaper and drinking coffee, Xander in his highchair next to him. Both grinned at her as she entered the room, and Patrick motioned to the chair beside him and busied himself getting a mug of coffee for his beloved wife. With her hair tousled, and a sleepy look on her face, he thought she had never looked so beautiful, and promptly told her. Sophia gave him a little smile, still groggy from the night's rest.

After a while of sitting mostly in silence as Sophia drank her first cup of coffee and Patrick continued to catch up on the news, Sophia went to check on Joel. She was quite nervous to do so, wanting so much to see an improvement, but worried that there wouldn't be one so quickly.

Sophia gently knocked on the bedroom door, and hearing no response, pushed the door open. The room was dark, but the light of the morning was beginning to push through the curtains, and she could just make Joel out, sleeping soundly. She tiptoed over to his side, bending down to look at his face, and could see that he appeared relaxed and at ease. What she also noticed was that he didn't look sweaty at all, although the room was quite warm, the radiators having come on for a couple of hours that morning. She gently touched his temple and found that he felt dry to the touch. She smiled to herself, knowing that he was going to be fine, and her heart swelled with love for her son. She knew that it was not going to be easy for him or Cassie in the coming weeks, but at least he had his health back, and for that, she was extremely grateful.

Hearing voices in the kitchen, she quickly retraced her steps, quietly shutting the bedroom door behind her so that Joel could continue sleeping and healing.

Martha had arrived through the back door as usual, and Sophia gave her a big hug in greeting.

'Gosh, you get earlier and earlier!' she teased her friend.

'I'm sorry,' Martha looked at her sheepishly, 'I was just up and wanted to see how Joel was.'

'I'm only teasing,' Sophia smiled at her friend, gently patting her arm. 'I've just checked on him and he's sleeping soundly. It's hard to tell at the moment, but he looks less sweaty so that's a good sign.'

Patrick looked up from his paper at them both, 'Why what happened last night?'

The two friends looked at each other as if they had just been caught doing something they shouldn't and Patrick gently folded up his paper as if ready for their explanation.

'Well…' started Sophia, and Martha helped herself to a fresh mug of coffee before making herself comfortable beside Xander.

'….and that's it really. I know this might be hard for you to understand, dear, it's been very difficult for me, but hopefully, Joel will now start to heal and feel a lot better.'

Sophia and Martha looked at Patrick with wide eyes, waiting for his reaction to the unbelievable events that they had recently experienced. There was a lengthy pause before Patrick said, 'How interesting. You should have told me all about it, I would have loved to have been there.'

Sophia gasped, 'Really?'

'Of course. I've always been interested in these things and often thought that Joel's anger was connected to a past life in some way, especially his birthmark. That's a common link, apparently. And then when you think about the soldiers and battles we enacted together, it seems likely doesn't it?'

'I'm shocked we haven't discussed this, dear,' Sophia said, looking at her husband in a quizzical way. 'I had no idea you believed in all this stuff.'

'Well, if you'd asked or, I guess, if I'd said, we would have known.' He smiled gently at his wife. 'That's a lesson for us too then. More communication.'

Sophia couldn't bring herself to speak but just nodded gently.

Suddenly, the kitchen door opened and the three of them looked up in unison.

'Morning everyone,' Joel said, padding into the kitchen. 'Is there enough coffee for me?'

'Xander! Hello gorgeous boy!' He ruffled his son's hair, bending down to give him a massive kiss. Xander giggled and threw his arms up to be lifted out of his seat. Joel raised him easily, swinging him into the air and making them both giggle again.

'Come and sit down,' Sophia said, 'before you tire yourself out again.' She patted the chair between her and Patrick while Patrick filled a mug of coffee and placed it on the counter.

Joel sat down, his son bouncing and giggling on his knee, and smiled at his parents.

'I feel much better today, and I'm not sweating either,' he said, puffing out his chest as if to show them his dry T-shirt.

'I'm glad to see you're better, son,' Patrick said, gently patting him on the shoulder and grinning at his grandson. 'It's a relief to have you back.'

'You do look much better,' Martha added, 'I'm so glad.' And

she also smiled at him, an image from her nanny life briefly flooding her mind.

'Thanks, Martha. You look lovely this morning by the way,' Joel added.

'Thank you!' Martha exclaimed. 'How nice to get such a compliment.'

'In fact, you both look beautiful,' Patrick added, to the ladies' complete surprise. 'Maybe this Red Magus of yours rejuvenated you both last night.'

The women laughed and Joel looked bemused at the comment.

Ava stared at herself in the mirror, her eyes wide with shock. She just didn't know what to do or how to feel. A wave of anxiety and sheer panic rose through her body, threatening to overwhelm her completely, and she found her breath becoming quicker and quicker, to the point that she could hardly breathe. She screwed up her face as she concentrated hard on slowing the gasps escaping from her small frame. As she did so, she shook her hands either side of her, as if this would also allow some of the emotion to escape through her fingertips. Eventually, as her breath began to slow and deepen, she sunk to the floor, her back against the cool tile of the bathroom wall. Ava continued to focus on her breathing for a good thirty minutes until she felt as if her body was able to relax a little, and for her breathing pattern to become more normal. She hugged her legs to her, sunk her head to her knees and began to sob. Gently at first, but quickly deepening to giant gasps that rocked her slight frame to its core. The emotion of the situation drained every ounce of strength from

Ava's body, and she slid down onto the floor, pulling a towel half under her head, and half over her body, closing her eyes as she did so. Within seconds she was asleep, as if her body and mind just needed to shut down for a while.

A couple of hours later, Ava woke shivering in the darkness. It took a few minutes to work out where she was, lying on the cold tile of her bathroom floor. Time had passed, and the light had faded, so it was not just cold but dark as well. She stiffly stumbled to her knees, and then her feet, heading straight for her large glamorous bed, sliding under the covers, still shivering, but wrapping herself in the thick duvet in a vain effort to get warm. As the warmth began to seep back into her limbs, Ava drifted again into sleep, although this time it was difficult and unsettled.

She could see her father standing at the end of a tunnel of light. His profile was unmistakable. He was wearing his army fatigues, his trousers tucked into his large heavy boots. His hands were on his waist in a power stance and his beret was pulled tight around his head. However, she could see his natural curls, highlighted against the light, just escaping around his ears. He would have hated that, she thought to her surprise. He hated his hair being curly and usually kept it extremely short to disguise his natural look. Why am I seeing that? Ava thought. Why is he here? she asked her subconscious. Instantly the image of her father morphed into a majestic eagle that swooped across her vision, making her physically duck as his talons became caught in her hair. Ava waved her arms over her head as if to bat the eagle away, and as she did so she woke with a jolt.

Whilst still on the fringes of sleep, Ava tried to sit up but was so cocooned in her duvet that, instead of it being a simple movement, it became a panicked fight of girl and duvet, until she eventually emerged, panting dramatically. As she allowed her eyes to focus on the familiarity of her bedroom, Ava's breath slowed, and she sunk back with an anguished cry. Seeing her father was never comfortable, yet somehow, this time, she felt as if he was trying to empower her and help her move forward. 'Ironic,' she said aloud to herself, 'he never helped me when he was here.'

The dream left her unsettled and she got out of bed, finding a snuggly lounge suit to put on. She didn't want to see anyone or go anywhere and just wanted to wear something warm and familiar to comfort her. Digging her feet into sheepskin slippers, she padded to the kitchen to make a hot drink. She felt totally disorientated and wasn't sure what time it was without checking the oversized kitchen clock. It was gone eleven at night but sleep now eluded her completely.

Ava made herself a herbal tea, something she would not normally drink, and selected from a choice of only three little sealed packets that she found in the cupboard. Ava couldn't even remember where they came from but one called 'Revitalise' drew her attention. She poured the boiling water carefully over the bag, the fact that she was pregnant whizzing back into her mind and shocking her afresh. She put the kettle down as if it was a lead weight, the tears stinging her eyes. Why was she so upset? She asked herself. It wasn't the end of the world. There were plenty of single mothers but she knew that she would never be one of them. She didn't want to bring a child into the world. Her experience of childhood had been harsh and difficult, and she didn't believe that she had it in her to be a kind and loving mother, which is what she had always craved. Her mother had been around but was so overpowered by her father, that her presence felt diluted somehow in Ava's mind. She had never stood up for Ava or surrounded her with cuddles and reassurance when her father had shouted and punished her. In fact, Ava wished she hadn't been there. It was easier not to have anyone rather than someone who did nothing.

Ava thought about Joel and whether she should tell him. After all, he had the right to know that he would have another child., But she knew that she couldn't. Joel would stay with his wife and firstborn, she knew that to the core of her being, and she would lose him in a spectacular failure for all to see. The tears came again but this time they were ones of humiliation.

Ava awoke still lying on her sofa, the early light starting to filter into the room. She lay listening to the birds singing their dawn chorus and started immediately going over her situation again in her head. She felt drained and exhausted, even though she had just woken up. She rolled onto her back and gently rubbed her stomach, questioning her feelings at that point, and deliberately picturing Joel as she did so. There was no usual flutter of excitement at the thought of him, instead, she felt irritated. He was weak, she thought. Maybe her father constantly in her dreams was trying to tell her that. He had hated any signs of weakness, and he would have hated Joel, she was sure. The memory of their night in a hotel when Joel woke with a start, and his birthmark seemed to throb in the darkness, came back to her vividly. She felt repulsed and, jumping up from the sofa, rushed to the bathroom to be sick.

The Healing

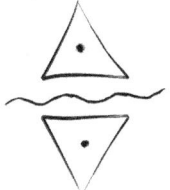

Cassie had expected to feel amazing after the session at Sara's, and the finality of it. The little group of friends had stopped the Magus from hurting Joel and had burned the effigy and the energetic intent that it held – to bind Ava and make her lose interest. They had basically saved her husband's life and made his mistress back off. They had then been treated to psychic phenomena courtesy of the Magus. They had been involved in the most extraordinary energy work, yet, when Cassie woke the next morning, she felt strange and out of sorts. It was almost as if she was coming down with a cold, but there was no mucus, just the headache, aches, and low energy.

She had carefully made her way downstairs for her first coffee of the morning, feeling very delicate and wobbly, whilst collecting her unicorn journal on the way. Cassie spent some time making notes on the previous evening's activities, while fully caffeinating herself in an effort to feel regenerated. However, it didn't really work, and she felt like going back to bed once she had finished. She wasn't collecting Xander for a couple of hours so decided to do just that to recover.

When she woke it was only an hour later and she felt no better. She knew she had to shower and collect Xander soon but just didn't feel like she could manage it. She reached for her phone to message Sophia, knowing that she would love to keep her son a little longer, and once an affirmative response was received, pulled the duvet back over her head.

When she woke for the second time, Cassie was surprised to see it was several hours later, and this time she did feel better. She slowly showered and dressed, still feeling a little weak and choosing to wear her most comfortable clothes, before setting out to pick up her son. When she arrived at Sophia and Patrick's house, Xander was having an afternoon nap, and Sophia was ready and waiting with a warm welcome.

Sophia and Cassie retreated to the conservatory with their mugs of tea and the baby monitor, while Patrick and Joel kept out of the way in the garden shed.

'Do you want to speak to Joel?' Sophia had enquired.

'Not really,' Cassie said, shaking her head. 'I feel really rough today. It must be the effect of last night. We will need to speak but I just don't feel up to it at the moment.'

'Well, it was a massive energetic shift for you both, wasn't it? Maybe you need some time to process,' Sophia offered. 'It will wait.'

Cassie nodded and pulled her blanket higher onto her lap. 'I just feel cold and out of sorts. Maybe I should check with Sara and see what she thinks.'

'Good idea,' Sophia agreed. 'If it reassures you, then give her a ring.'

Cassie picked up her mobile phone and was soon chatting with Sara as to her opinion. Sara was sure that it was the effect of the energy work they had done. It was quite common for people to feel worse before they felt better, as the energy shifted, and the information and realisations were processed. Sara recommended that Cassie do as little as possible, drink lots of water, sleep, and be kind to herself.

They agreed to check in again with each other in a week to make sure everything was back to normal. However, Cassie didn't feel any better when they next spoke and Sara encouraged her to come for another session. There was obviously something blocking the integration and they needed to investigate further.

'Thanks for seeing me,' Cassie hugged her friend a welcome. 'I just feel completely off, as if I'm not quite in my body.'

'Well, that's a possibility. Maybe a part of you wanted to stay with the Red Magus and her world.'

'Maybe?' Cassie queried. 'I'm not aware that I did that, but it definitely doesn't feel normal.'

'Well, let's find out what it is. Why don't you settle down on the cushions and we'll see where the energy takes us.'

Almost as soon as she had got comfortable, and the intention for the session had been set, Cassie began to speak.

'I can see the queue again. The line of my ancestors behind me.' There was a slight pause before she excitedly and a bit incredulously said, 'And now in front of me. I'm being shown my future lives as well.'

Sara smiled and shook her head slightly in wonderment,

leaning forward towards Cassie to better hear what she was saying.

'The line is beginning to morph now. Instead of there being many characters behind me, and in front of me in a straight line, they are forming a shape, like a pattern around me. It's like a cobweb with each intersection having a character on it.'

There was a pause and then Cassie explained, 'It represents my Soul Continuum, that Soul essence that travels on through time and space, and can never be destroyed, only changed in some way. Each character that I can see is the possibility for a life and Soul growth, by developing the skills that I have in that lifetime, or by fully understanding an emotion from all aspects, or by stepping fully into my power. They are all lessons of growth. This lifetime is as well. Forgiveness and empowerment.'

'Can you see whether the energy between you is completely integrated?' Sara asked.

There was a pause as Cassie concentrated on the question and what she was seeing in her mind's eye. 'I don't think it is. I think that's why I feel so out of sorts. There's something stopping the integration between the Magus and me, on our strand of the cobweb, but I'm not sure what.'

Cassie's brow furrowed slightly as Sara intently watched her, waiting for her to speak again.

There was a very long pause, and whilst Sara waited, she channelled Reiki to her friend and client, hoping that the beautiful energy would highlight the blockage and help the process.

Eventually, Cassie said, 'I think it's about me fully understanding and accepting that this lifetime or reality is such a small part of our Soul Continuum. It's such a small part of the dimensions that we can go to energetically, and yet that is little understood.'

Sara paused not only her movement but also her breath, holding both with fascination as she waited for Cassie to speak again.

'There are so many worlds and dimensions that we can travel to, to find guidance and understanding, and to support other aspects of ourselves in their learnings. Anyone can do what I have done with the Magus, anyone can connect to another lifetime and work together with that aspect of their Soul energy, for the highest and best outcome.'

Sara nodded at her friend, as she tried to fully take this information in. 'How exciting that we know that now, and we can work on connecting to those aspects or parts of our Soul energy that need our help.'

'I think there's something else though. It doesn't look quite right,' Cassie added.

Sara stopped giving the Reiki and sat back on the sofa, so she could fully concentrate. 'What doesn't look right?' she queried.

'There are splinters in the strand between us,' Cassie announced.

'Splinters? Splinters of what?'

'I think they are energy splinters. That's what they look like. Little barbs, like thorns but glowing as if opalescent. They're not white though, they look dark.'

'I wonder if it's psychic attack?' Sara offered, almost to herself.

'What's that?' Cassie asked, opening her eyes, and turning her head to look at Sara.

'It's negative thoughts or words that somebody has thrown at you, like little poisoned darts. Sometimes they do it deliberately, but a lot of the time it's unconscious. Maybe Joel and Ava have sent them your way? After all, you were sending negative energy their way as well.'

Cassie looked up at the ceiling, her eyes wide open, as she contemplated this information. 'Yes, I can see that. They must have had a few negative thoughts towards the source of their discomfort, whether they knew who or what that was.'

'Exactly,' Sara nodded. 'Why don't you connect with one of the splinters and see what information you get.'

Cassie closed her eyes and concentrated on one of the little barbs, the image of which grew larger as if her focusing on it was magnifying it in her mind's eye. Once enlarged, she could see images within it of faces and mouths, screaming and shouting. 'It's anger,' she stated. 'It's barbs of anger that have got caught in my Soul Continuum.'

Sara nodded, 'Of course. That makes perfect sense. Why don't you ask your Guide how we can clear them?'

'Send love and light to them,' Cassie stated and went quiet again. Sara knew she was doing just that and joined her sending the beautiful loving energy of Reiki to her friend. Sara knew it would amplify whatever Cassie was able to send, although her friend was so powerful now that Sara didn't believe for one second that she couldn't do it herself. However, Sara wanted to be there for Cassie and to back up her efforts.

'They are slowly dissolving,' Cassie eventually said, 'and the whole of my Soul Continuum is lighting up as if they had been stopping the energy from flowing. It feels energising and empowering.' Cassie smiled, 'Exactly what I needed.'

'That's great,' Sara added. 'Is there anything else that we need to look at?' She waited for Cassie to reply.

Sara expected Cassie to be ready to finish the session, so she was a bit surprised when Cassie said, 'There is something else that's bothering me.'

'Tell me what you see,' Sara invited, sitting back on the sofa.

'The Magus doesn't look quite right. She looks unkempt, and her hair looks dirty and untidy. I saw her in a dream ages ago looking like this, as if something was happening to her in her lifetime that was a real struggle for her.' Cassie paused, her face one of concern. 'I can't get what is happening to her, but something is and she's now struggling. I suppose I've been struggling in my life recently, and I think it's the same for her, but it feels ominous.' Cassie paused again and Sara calmly waited for her to continue. 'I'm scared for her,' Cassie finally said.

'Can you get any more information?' Sara asked, equally concerned for this character that she had grown so fond of. 'Can you sense what has been happening to her?'

'No. I feel as if it's blocked. As if she's not allowing me to have that information for some reason. Maybe it's not time for me to see that.'

'Well, I have no doubt that you will over time. Do you want to end the session?'

'Yes, I think that is all I can get at the moment,' Cassie concluded.

Over the following days, Cassie felt her energy increase and her cold symptoms subside. She not only felt physically stronger but emotionally empowered as well. She had been putting off speaking to Joel but knew that the time would come when they would need to decide how they were going to move forward, and whether that would be together or alone.

However, whenever Cassie thought of her life in the future, Joel was not there. Somehow through the last few months, her love for him had changed, from that of an infatuated wife to now just a kind and compassionate friend. She knew without a doubt that they had been destined to meet in this life, to work out their karma from their lives before, but she also knew that there were no energetic cords between them anymore. The help that the Magus had sent her way had cleared anything left for them to resolve, and the result was a change in her energy and in the future of her current life. Somehow the events of the last few months had altered her path in this lifetime, and what lay ahead had yet to be written. This need to alter course was new and unexpected, and where it would lead her, she had no idea, but she was filled with excitement and optimism. Cassie knew it wasn't going to be easy, but she felt so different now and was sure that what was to come would be life-enhancing. To start that new path, and with newfound empowerment, she started to make plans for herself.

Cassie had spoken to Sara to organise some more regular sessions, so she could keep connecting with her Soul Continuum, and into the many lives where lessons had yet to be completed. Her plan was to help those parts of her as much as possible, to see where it would lead them all, and how they could move towards living their highest potential. She also wanted to find out why the Magus appeared to be struggling, and what was happening to her in her lifetime. Cassie knew that there was another chapter to that life that she had to help resolve, and she itched to start the process. Cassie also wanted Sara to teach her Reiki and crystal healing, so that she could start to build on her knowledge as much as possible. Sara, of course, had happily agreed to all her friend's requests. She loved working with Cassie and knew that their path would be a fascinating one, pushing at the edges of what was possible in energy work.

Cassie had also spoken to Sophia and Patrick and asked that they still be in her life. She saw them as her parents and couldn't bear the thought that what had happened in her marriage would affect their friendship and love. Unsurprisingly, they vowed to support her no matter what and to be around for Xander whenever Cassie needed their help. In fact, they had organised a couple of days during the week when Xander would stay with them, to build on the loving relationship that was already there, and to give Cassie some space to forge a new life. They already knew that she would leave Joel. It broke their hearts but they were determined to be supportive of Cassie and their grandson whenever required.

Cassie had also spoken to Martha, who she felt equally connected to. She wanted Martha to be around for her and to teach her everything she knew about connecting with Spirit. Martha was thrilled to have such a talented student, and they too had arranged sessions to kick-start their lessons. Cassie made sure that Martha knew how much she appreciated her love and support, and how much she was looking forward to working with her.

Cassie also knew it was time to speak to Joel and explain that she wanted a divorce. Just the word made her stomach flip but she now had reserves of courage and empowerment to draw on and she knew that she was making the right decision. She wanted Joel to be around for Xander, and with the support of Patrick and Sophia, she knew that it would be possible. Joel adored his son and he was a good father and, for that, Cassie was extremely grateful. However, his betrayal had changed her feelings towards him and churned them into a platonic state. Joel was devastated to finally hear those words but not surprised, and they promised each other that they would work together as much as possible to support Xander in his life.

Finally, Cassie spoke to the Magus. She was incredibly fond of this part of her and awed by the power she could feel from her whenever she checked in. She knew that the time would come when their energies and images would be morphed, and the face of the Magus would be lost to her, but she also knew that there was more they needed to work on together. Whenever Cassie checked in, and often in her dreams, she could feel that the Magus was struggling. There was a great deal of fear and anxiety and whenever she appeared in Cassie's mind's eye, she looked thin and unkempt. Cassie knew that she had to help this part of her now. The Magus had helped her, and now it was her time to do the rescuing. That power had been transferred from one lifetime to another so that they could help each other. But she was frightened too. The tendrils of fear that flowed from the Magus from across time and space were strong and wound their way into Cassie's dreams and thoughts. Cassie was aware that they were not her anxieties and became very impatient to start the process so that she could clear them, but she was apprehensive as well. Tendrils of her own fear would also come and go but she now had the strength to push them away. She also knew that her friends would be there to help her if need be, and she decided to share what was happening with them again. This time, Patrick was also to be included, as he clearly had hidden knowledge and skills that she might need to use.

Cassie was excited about what was to happen next. She felt empowered for the first time in her life and that gave her freedom. She was free to do whatever she wanted, go wherever she wanted, and learn whatever subject called to her. She was also free to travel energetically into many different worlds and that prospect excited and enthralled her. She was ready for the next adventure.

The End

About the Author

Natasha Joy Price is an Energy Therapist, teacher and author. She runs her own business, Dandelion Therapies, and is passionate about energy work. Natasha believes that we should all be working on our energy field daily, to shift old emotions, beliefs, and perspectives. Her mission is to help her clients learn ways to clear and clean their energy and find a more balanced and centred approach to life. Natasha's first book, *Freedom of the Soul*, was written as a proactive energy management workbook to help her readers discover their own spiritual paths. Natasha has studied many energy healing modalities including Past Life Regression Therapy, Reiki, Crystal Healing, Theta Healing, and her own Soul Continuum Healing. Natasha is also the host of the *Balm to the Soul* podcast, which has over a hundred episodes discussing all sorts of different energetic practices.

To learn more, visit www.dandeliontherapies.co.uk

www.ingramcontent.com/pod-product-compliance
Lightning Source LLC
Chambersburg PA
CBHW072046110526
44590CB00018B/3061